A Guide to Floral Mechanics

Published in the UK

Design by Sarah Diligent and William Mazuch

Text by Sarah Diligent and William Mazuch

Illustration by William Mazuch

Portrait illustrations by Sophia O'Connor

This 1st edition published 2020

A CIP catalogue record for this book is available from the British Library

ISBN 978-1-8380337-0-5

Sustainably printed in Great Britain on paper which is sourced from well managed forests and is FSC® certified. The printer and the manufacturing mill are both credited ISO14001 Environmental Management Systems Standard and are both FSC® certified.

FSC www.fsc.org MIX Paper from responsible sources FSC® C012830

A Guide to Floral Mechanics

by

Sarah Diligent

William Mazuch

foreword by

Shane Connolly

Preface

It seems clear that the world is changing; we are producing more waste and leaving a bigger carbon footprint than ever before; we are using more of the planet's resources than is sustainable. The floristry industry – at its very core a celebration of the natural world – can and must do better.

We have no interest in preaching or telling anyone what they must or ought to do. None of us is perfect. We are both as fallible as anyone else. Our aim with this book is to share the knowledge that we have discovered and developed over the years.

We believe that knowledge is power, and that at heart we all want to do the right thing. With realistic options set out in clear, straightforward steps we hope that this book will encourage and equip florists, students, flower arrangers, and flower lovers to make sustainable choices.

Floristry is changing, and we hope to encourage people to look at their own practices, and to ask themselves what more they can do. If readers embrace the ethos of this book, leading to less waste, a smaller carbon footprint and fewer resources being used, then the book will have been a success. Nature is extraordinary. Let's celebrate it considerately and sustainably. If we don't, who will? If not now, then when? We hope that this book will inspire you as much as writing it has inspired us.

As a reference manual, this book is written to be a guide of sorts, and the reader shouldn't feel obliged to read it from cover to cover.

The support from individuals across the world in bringing this book to print has been astounding. The trust placed in us has been humbling and we hope that this guide holds the answers that you are looking for.

Sarah & William

Foreword

Shane Connolly

Floral designer and Royal Warrant holder

For an industry with its roots so firmly in nature, the flower trade has held a poor track record in environmental matters over the last few decades.

A design-led ethos has dominated much of the business, where the end result is more important than the means of achieving it; design at any cost and, in essence, design without responsibility.

But I think there has been a noticeable sea change in the last few years, and floral designers are becoming increasingly aware of the word 'sustainability'.

With awareness comes responsibility and confusion too.
Those of us who try to work thoughtfully are constantly being asked: 'How can we change the way we have been taught?' and 'How do we learn how to work sustainably?'

I think the answers start with a question:

WHY did we choose to work with flowers in the first place?
The answer is usually the love of flowers and then the connection with nature, and the need to protect her at all costs, become blindingly obvious.

Working seasonally and sourcing flowers and foliage responsibly is a good starting point.

But the physical practicalities of HOW to use these flowers and how to design using sustainable methods, while still retaining one's own unique style, are still insurmountable obstacles for many floral designers.

And this is why I think this book by Sarah Diligent and William Mazuch is so important.

They have looked at the technical challenges of floral designs and given clear, concise and sustainable methods for achieving them.

Sarah's floral experience and flair combine with William's design background to give a unique and foolproof manual of simple, practical methodology that can be learnt, adapted, perhaps improved and certainly, made specific to each designer and design.

It has been written without the ego of a particular floral style or look which would distract from the importance of the physical mechanics.

And William's simple, precise drawings bring a clarity that is absent in almost all other books on floral technique.

So the end product is comprehensive, clear and easy to use.

I am honoured to write the foreword to this book as I think it will become a vehicle for change for the whole industry. It will help those who want to make a difference learn how to actually do so and help make sustainable floral design an achievable goal for floral designers at every level.

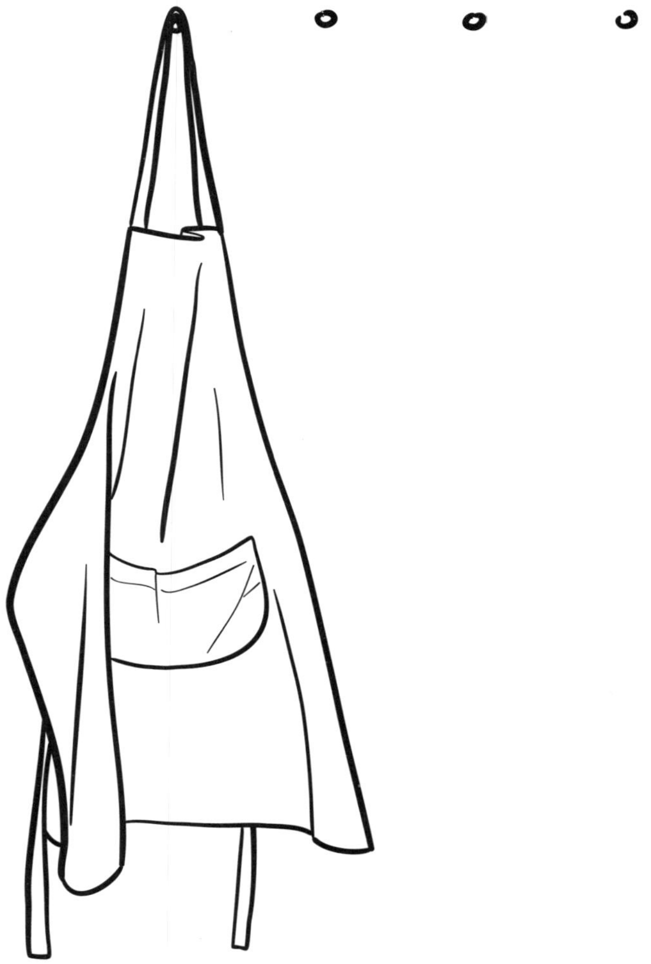

fig.1

Contents

Introduction

A Guide to Floral Mechanics has been written to share with you the methods that we use in our studio in Hampshire. We work in the most sustainable ways we can, eliminating single-use plastics wherever possible, reusing and recycling as much as we can. We don't want to tell you how you must work, just how we do. If that works for you too, then we'll be delighted.

This book is a manual and a guide for reference. As long as you have read the section on conditioning (page 15), or already have a good understanding of it, you do not need to read the book in its entirety, or even in order.

Our style of floristry is naturalistic, embracing the wildness of stems and the nuances of seasonal blooms, but the methods outlined in this book are suited to work in all styles, no matter how relaxed or formal. Over the years we have developed and tested both old and new techniques, always aiming to lower our carbon footprint without compromising on quality. Being eco-friendly shouldn't have to be a trade-off.

Our approach may differ from the way that you usually work, or there may be great swathes of crossover. Either way, we hope that the mechanics within this book will give you more freedom to create and that it will inspire rather than inhibit. We hope that the carbon footprint of floristry will shrink as people realise that working more sustainably isn't such a huge shift, and that designing in a manner which considers the ramifications of our work is worth the effort.

This is not a book on floral design. It is a guide to how we create the mechanics which form the base of floral designs. There are a few exceptions to this rule though; simple, neutral floral designs are outlined in the instructions for designs in which the stems of the flowers and foliage become the mechanics. When referring to 'floral mechanics' we are talking about the supplies, methods and materials used to place and hold stems of flowers and foliage within a floral design.

Our intention is to show through imagery and instructions how to create, without being prescriptive about design. Our hope is that by sharing our methods, we will not influence your style, but will extend your options.

The mechanics we outline over the next hundred pages or so can accommodate a range of styles and take little, if any, longer than other methods to complete, while being reusable and inexpensive with minimal use of single-use plastics. We endeavour to show that alternatives to single-use plastics can and do work. There is still, however, one single-use plastic used in the studio: pot tape. Occasionally we use pot tape, and while we're working on alternatives to it, we've not found anything quite strong enough to replace it yet. The more we change, the more we realise there is that we can do. Each change might seem insignificant on its own, but we believe that these differences add up and together are worth the effort.

Despite avoiding single-use plastics wherever possible we have nothing against using reusable plastic. We do in fact use plastic items in many forms. From buckets to window planters and plastic packaging, we would rather use things that already exist and reuse them as many times as possible. It is a part of living in the twenty-first century. There is a lot of plastic around and we would rather use what exists until it has been exhausted than send it to landfill unused.

One plastic we do avoid entirely is floral foam, which can be washed into waterways and it is not biodegradable. We have not used floral foam in the studio since 2015 and have never had to turn down a job as a result of not using foam.

Tools

It is worth buying good tools and looking after them. Your hands will be grateful and your work will be easier. The tools outlined in the following pages are either needed to create the mechanics in this guide or make creating them easier.

1. Floristry scissors. Use whichever you're comfortable with. Japanese floristry scissors are great to work with and are readily available online.

2. A sharpener. A two-in-one tungsten and diamond sharpener works on knives, scissors, secateurs and loppers.

3. Measuring tape. Essential for measuring things both in the studio and off site.

4. Gloves. A pair of leather gloves for handling branches and sharp or spiky plant material. Also useful for handling chicken wire.

5. Pliers. Long-nose pliers are an important part of a kit bag, and will be useful in more scenarios than you might expect.

6. Loppers. Essential for responsible foraging and for cutting through larger branches.

7. Fabric/ribbon scissors. Used for fabrics, ribbons and hook-and-loop strapping (Velcro). Any fabric scissors will suffice. Keep solely for use with fabrics.

8. Knitting needle, spike or skewer. Used for making guide holes for flowers and for adding foliage to densely packed moss.

9. Wire cutters. Used for cutting chicken wire, reel wire and stub wires.

10. Secateurs. A good pair of sharp secateurs is invaluable.

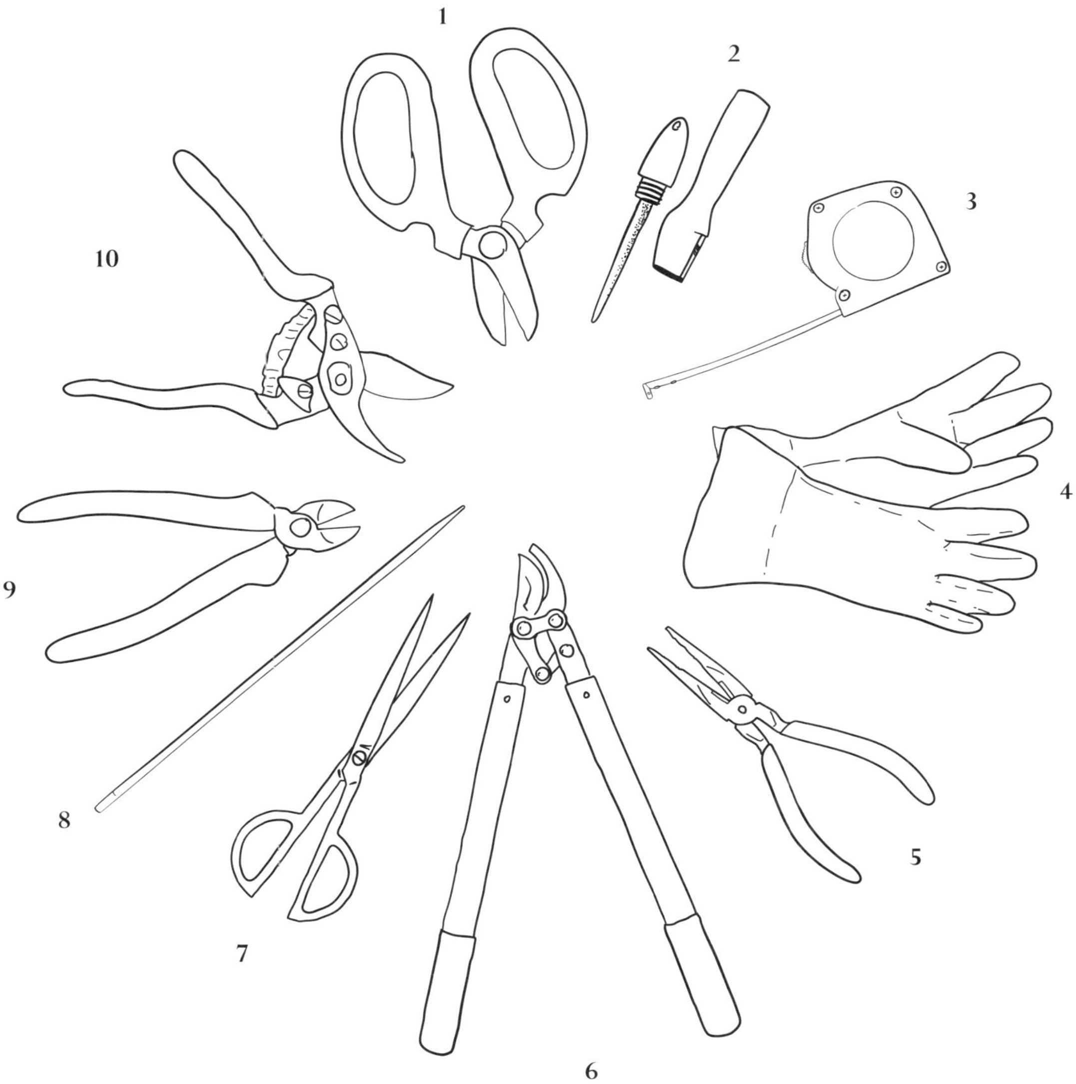
1
2
3
4
5
6
7
8
9
10

Equipment and Sundries

Equipment refers to the elements of a florist's toolbox that will have to be replaced every so often, which you will get more than one use from and are likely to be able to re-use after an event.

Sundries are items that will need replenishing from time to time. These are consumables, and as such you are unlikely to be able to reuse them when an event is over.

1. Apron. (fig.1, page ii) A protective garment covering the front of one's clothes which is often tied at the back.

2. Moss. There are many different types of moss. We recommend using sustainably sourced grass moss. In situations where vessels cannot be filled with water, particularly for wreaths and funeral work, moss can be used to keep flowers and foliage hydrated.

3. Kenzan/pin holders/frogs. These come in many shapes and sizes and are made in a variety of materials. It is worth noting that not all of these are rustproof.

4. Turntable/Lazy Susan. A revolving stand or tray used for turning designs while creating, which saves you from having to walk around the workbench to get an overview.

5. Twine. Invaluable for creating biodegradable funeral work, and useful for tying off floral designs such as bouquets, pew ends and buttonholes.

6. Paper-covered wire. Usually in brown or green, but available in many colours. Sometimes called bindwire, useful for binding, securing plant materials and securing elements in larger designs.

7. Pot tape. This strong, plastic tape is usually green or clear and is strong enough to secure chicken wire to vessels. It can also be used to create grids.

8. Metal wreath ring. Reusable metal ring typically mossed to create a base for wreaths.

9. Waxed floral tape. Also known as Stemtex tape, gutta percha, or, stem wrap, this biodegradable tape is made of crepe paper covered in a soft wax. It is a self-sealing tape most commonly found in green and is used for securing and sealing flowers and foliage in installations, buttonholes, corsages, flower crowns and bouquets.

10. Hook-and-loop strapping (Velcro). This back-to-back fabric strapping is strong, washable and reusable, sticks to itself and can be used in place of cable ties. (Cut to length with fabric scissors.)

11. Floral fix/tack. A reusable adhesive wax/tack used for fixing elements such as kenzan onto vessels.

12. Fishing line. This plastic string comes in various strengths and is used for suspended installations such as floral clouds where mechanics for suspension should be as close to invisible as possible.

2

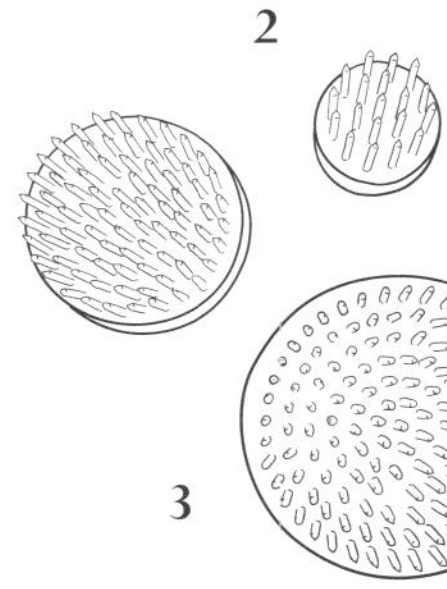

3

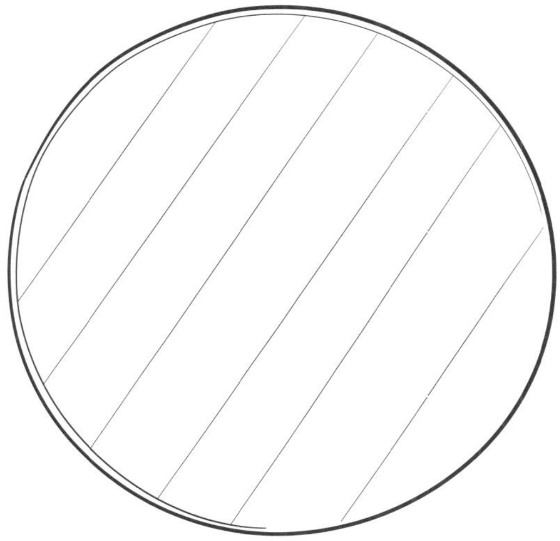

4

5

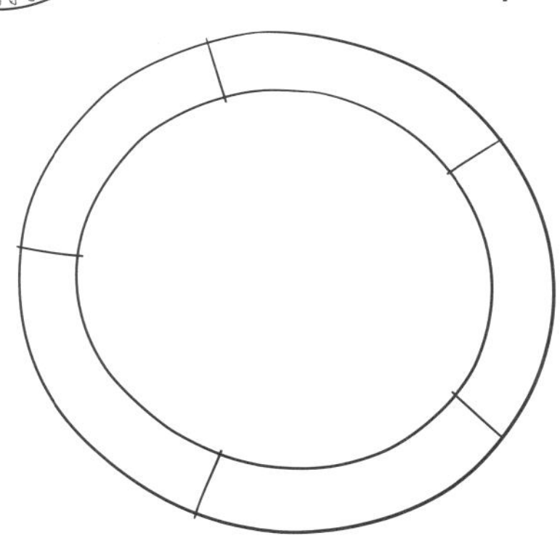

8

6

7

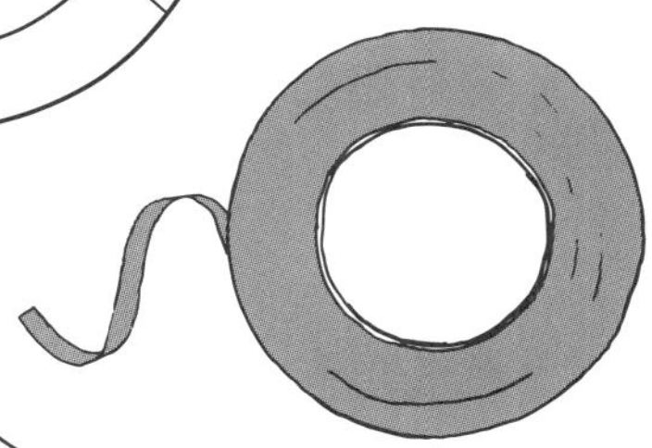

9

10

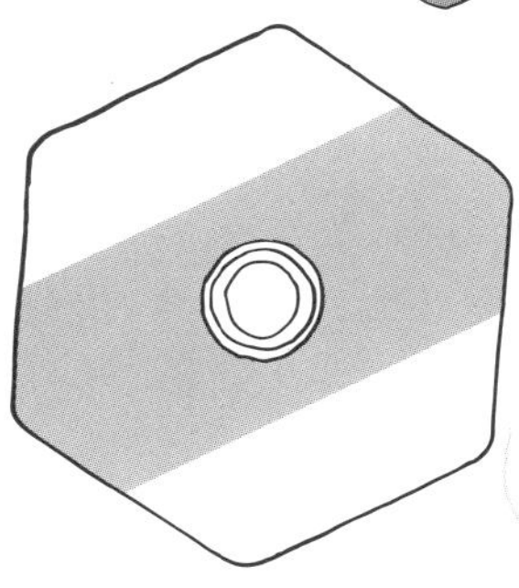

11

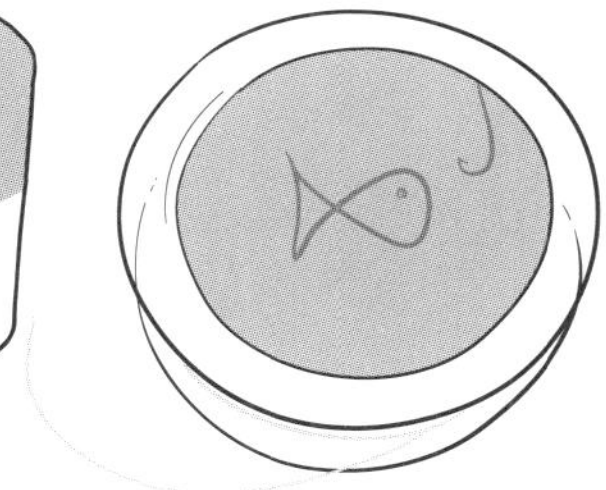

12

13. Stub wires. Typically used by florists to support delicate elements, these come in a number of gauges. The higher the gauge number, the thinner the wire.

14. Pins. Metal pins, pearl pins or glass-headed pins are invaluable for pinning buttonholes and corsages to garments. We do not use magnets due to the risk of interaction with pacemakers.

15. Ribbons. Often the finishing touch for bouquets. While frequently they are synthetic, natural materials such as cotton, silk and bamboo silk (a vegan product) are available. Ribbons made from natural products are usually biodegradable and are often dyed with natural dyes.

16. Test tubes. Also known as florist's stem tubes, floral water tubes, and, flower vials. These come in different sizes and colours, often supplied with caps. Replacement caps can be bought separately.

17. Reel wire. This is also known as florist's wire, binding wire, and, mossing wire. It has a multitude of uses.

18. Carabiner. A shackle or coupling link with safety closure used when suspending hanging installations.

19. Blow torch. Used to sear the stem ends of flowers such as poppies. There are many types of blowtorch available, with flame control, non-slip handles and refillable cylinders. The small varieties are useful for conditioning poppies if you have a large amount to prepare. If you are only conditioning small amounts, the flame from a lighter is adequate.

20. Camellia oil. Used for protecting and cleaning the blades of scissors, secateurs and loppers as well as knives and wire cutters.

21. Grave spike. A strong reusable plastic cone shaped vase with a spiked end.

22. Candle. Dinner candles, tea light candles and pillar candles can be used to add colour, scent and (of course) light.

23. Chicken wire. Options for chicken wire include uncoated, plastic-coated, and copper floral mesh. Chicken wire is reusable. Plastic-coated options will not degrade in landfill whereas metal wire is recyclable and will rust in time. 20-gauge chicken wire with a 25mm or 1-inch aperture (hole size) is ideal for the designs outlined in this guide.

24. Fabric. Used as a cover for planks in natural funeral work, brilliant for backdrops and good for placing in between a vessel and liner in large designs such as urn arrangements to ease separating the two after events. Another fabric we advise using is an oilcloth when working with moss, as it can prove messy.

25. Plank. Planks of wood cut into appropriate lengths are used as a biodegradable base for Coffin Toppers and as the base for Floral Clouds.

26. Non-slip mat. This comes in many variants, it is often washable and can be reused. Useful to keep floral designs in place, particularly funeral work.

27. Weights. Cast-iron Christmas tree stands make great weights for arches and installations. Poles or branches can also be added to quick-setting concrete in buckets to form weighted uprights. Stage weights can also be useful for weighing down structures as needed.

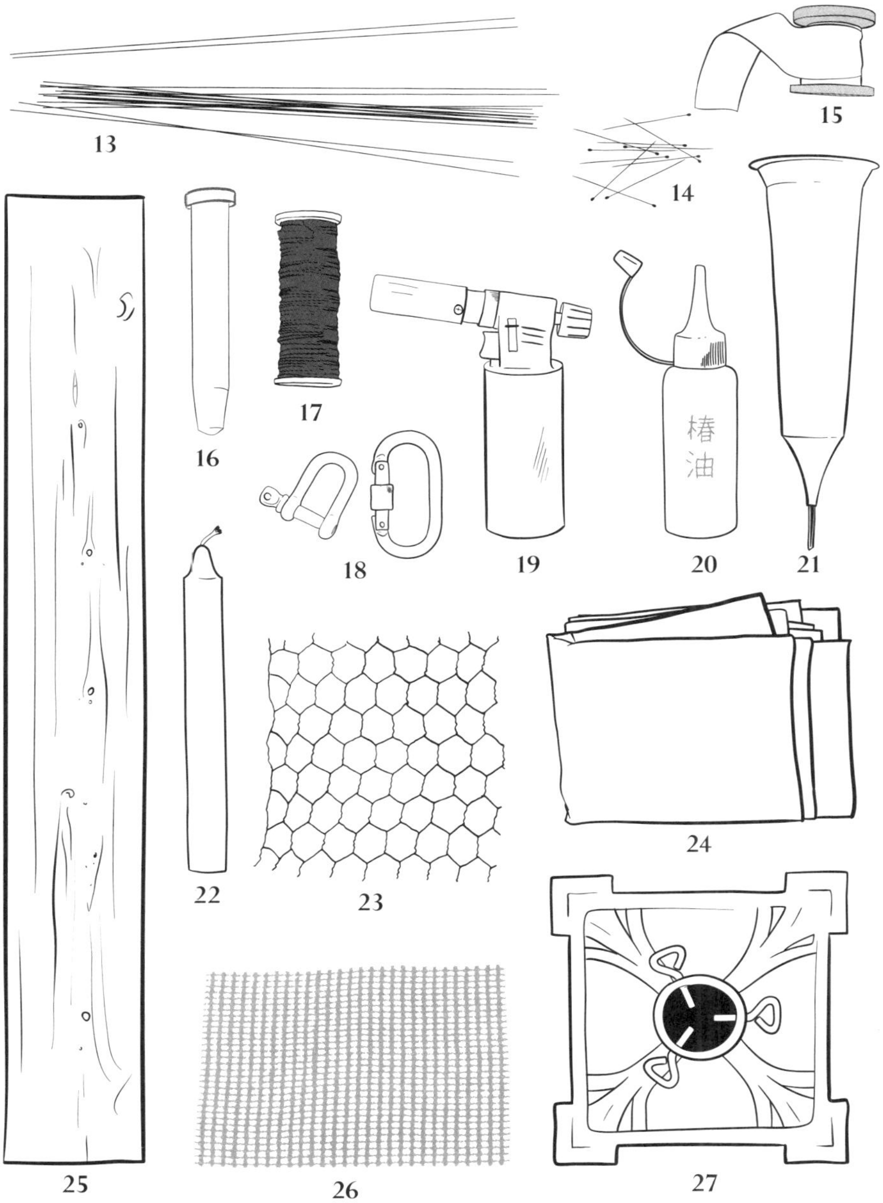
13
15
14
17
16
19
20
21
18
椿油
22
23
24
25
26
27

28. **Willow.** A natural and flexible material which can be manipulated into a variety of shapes and used as a base for floral designs. This is particularly useful for biodegradable wreaths and funeral work that needs to be entirely biodegradable. It should be noted that natural burial sites do not usually allow the use of any wires or plastics such as floral foam or plastic tapes.

29. **Water spray.** Used for misting finished designs and hydrating Kokedama.

30. **Dutch market style bucket.** These square-based buckets are useful for transportation thanks to their stability and have collars/necks which can be useful for supporting longer stems. Any stable buckets will be useful if Dutch market style buckets are unavailable.

31. **Water jug.** Used to fill vessels with water before arranging, top up the level of water in arrangements, or used as an informal vessel.

32. **Metal stand.** These come in a number of heights and can be used for elevated table designs and can also be used as plinths.

33. **Museum wax.** A reusable adhesive wax/tack used for fixing elements such as Kenzan onto vessels.

34. **Watering can.** It is useful to have a large watering can for topping up larger designs and a small watering can for adding water to smaller arrangements.

35. **Palm leaf tray.** Biodegradable trays which can be used to hold water and moss.

36. **Round bucket.** These are of course handy for holding water and for putting flowers and foliage in, and are invaluable when cut down to make vessel liners. They can also be placed upside down and used to elevate vessels when working on designs such as tall table centres.

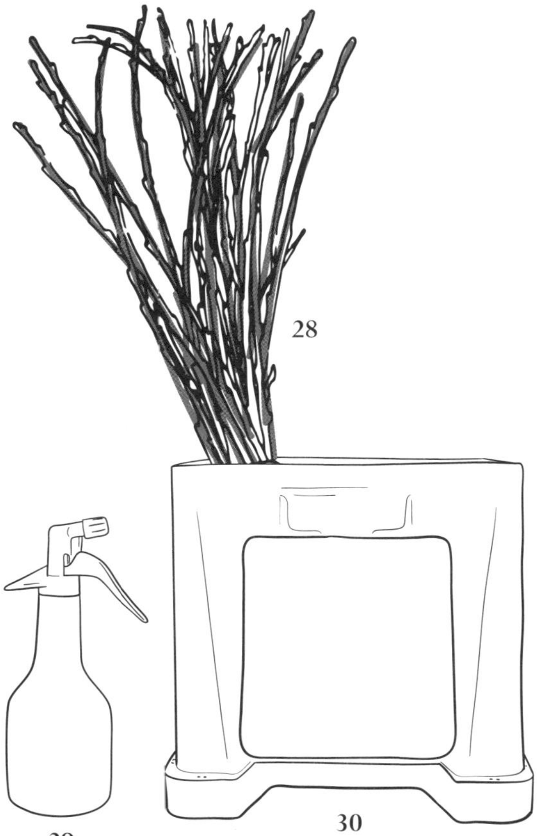

28

29

30

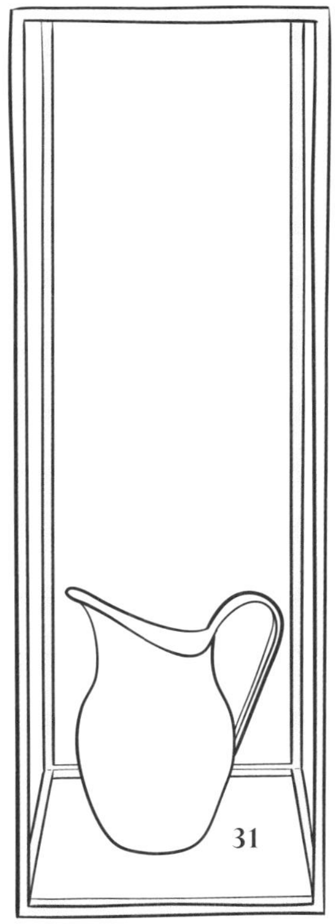

31

32

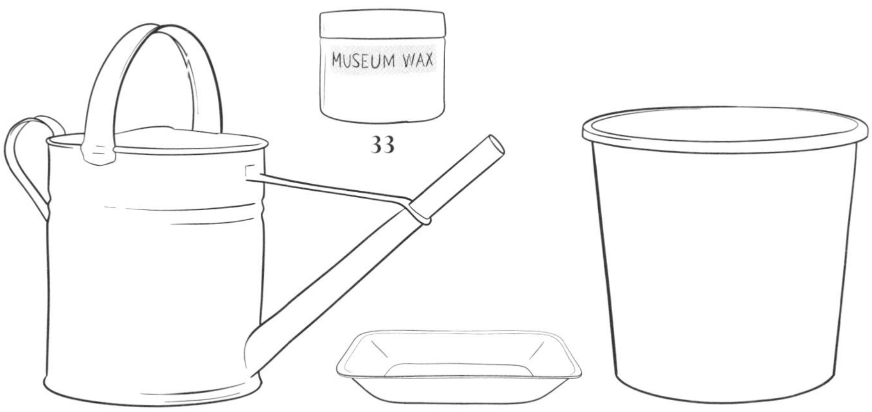

33

34

35

36

Vessels

Just about anything watertight can become a vessel, and even things which are not watertight can become a vessel if you insert a watertight liner and keep it stable. Cut down buckets can become inserts for large urns, bottles can hold water inside vases and biodegradable bags can be used as liners for short term designs.

Vessels are an integral part of most floral design, and your choice of shape, size and style will influence your end result.

1. Bottle-neck vase. The narrow neck and wide body of this vessel provide a large water source, good stability and support for single, statement stems.

2. Compote dish/pedestal/footed vase. Flowers and foliage are arranged in this type of vessel using a support system such as chicken wire, a kenzan, or a willow armature.

3. Rose bowl. These (often glass) bowls usually come with a made-to-measure grid and are designed to display roses *en masse* though they can be used for any flowers. Weighting flowers evenly through the design ensures stability.

4. Lotus vase. Most are ceramic, and are available in a range of sizes and colours. They are best suited to flowers with shorter, wider stems, as they tend to be shallow. A lotus vase can be difficult to clean.

5. Flower bowl. Typically a ceramic dish or bowl used with a kenzan or with chicken wire to support stems for table-centres or small arrangements.

6. Square or rectangular vases. Stems tend to fall into corners of these vases unless a grid or a large amount of material is used to stabilise elements. Square Vases can be useful for flowers such as hydrangea and roses which have large heads if you are looking to create a uniform design

7. Jug. Shorter rounder jugs work well for posies and gathered bunches of informal flowers. Tall straight versions are better for taller, straighter flowers such as sunflowers, snapdragons, lilac and foxgloves.

8. Jam jars. Suited to informal designs, jam jars require a lot of material to fill them due to their relatively wide necks. They can be used inside other vessels as a water source, and can be used for delivering gift bouquets in.

9. Cylinder or column vase. These versatile vessels come in a multitude of heights and widths. They are useful for designs using taller, straighter flowers and foliage.

10. Milk bottle vase. These have a wide mouth and a narrow neck, they are typically used for informal floral designs using just a few stems.

11. Tall floor standing vase. Used for larger flowers and branches. Often with narrow openings these are heavy, stable, statement pieces which suit designs comprising oversize elements.

12. Window planter/Trough. These are often made from durable plastic or terracotta, but can also be metal or fibreglass. What is important is that yours is watertight or can be lined. These become heavy when filled.

13. Low dish. Useful for elevated designs and to float flowers in, these come in many variants.

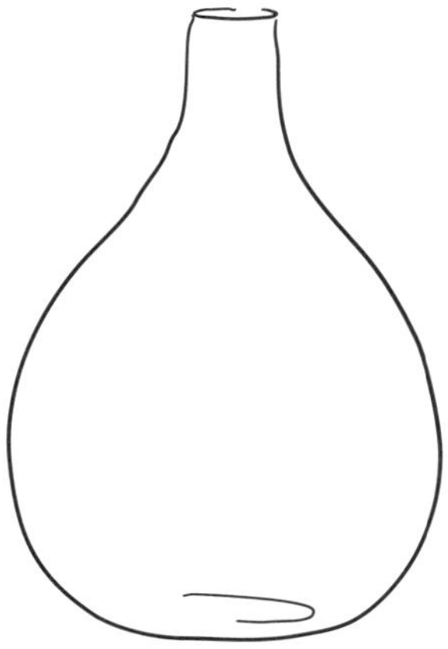
1

2

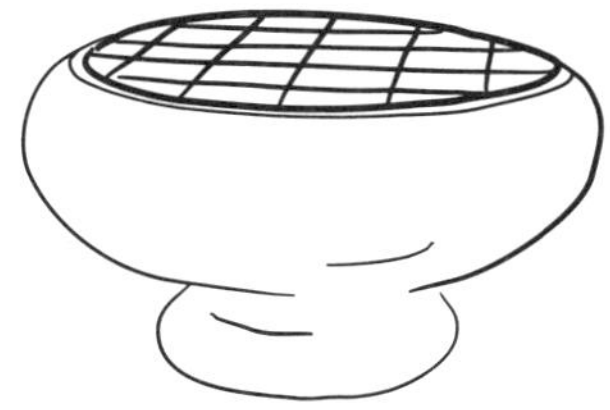
3

4

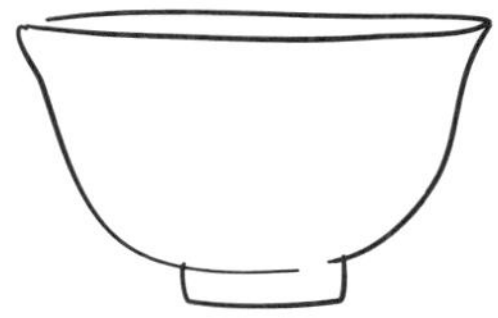
5

6

7

8

9

10

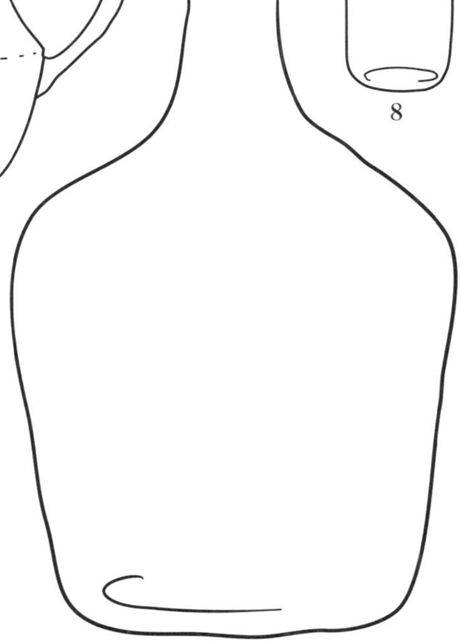
11

12

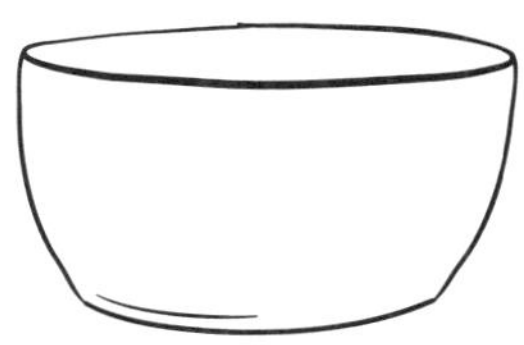
13

14. **Hurricane vase.** Often used for table centres and hallway designs. Typically a pillar candle is placed inside the vase which is surrounded by a garland or a wreath. These can also be used as a vase for larger arrangements, or bouquets with longer stems.

15. **Tapered vase.** This style of vase lends itself to more minimal floral design due to its narrow neck.

16. **Hourglass/bouquet vase.** The form of this vase makes it stable. Further mechanics are unnecessary as stems will naturally splay out to follow the shape of the vessel. It holds hand-tied posies and bouquets well as it mirrors their shape.

17. **Round/bowl vase.** This shaped vase is best suited to low arrangements where the stems are cut so that the blooms sit at the lip of the vase. It is also used in designs where blooms are submerged.

18. **Flared vase.** Suited to displays of larger headed flowers such as tulips, daffodils, and amaryllis due to the narrow base and wide opening.

19. **Bud vases.** For smaller designs single blooms or foliage sprigs. Often grouped together for effect.

20. **Constance Spry style ceramic vase/mantel vase.** These tend to be low, wide, shallow vessels, some have the original grids intact, if not, they will require the addition of mechanics such as a kenzan, chicken wire, or a willow armature to support stems.

21. **Small dish.** These small, shallow, ceramic dishes are ideal for ikebana-style arrangements. They typically contain just a kenzan and a little water, so need topping up regularly.

22. **Flower brick.** Traditionally ceramic and intended to be seen with the long side facing forward. Stems are arranged into the holes in the top. Some varieties have removable top sections which make for easier cleaning; in others this is fixed. They are related to the bough pot and tulipiere which have fewer holes and tend to be rounder.

23. **Urn/pedestal.** Typically ceramic or metal, these come in a multitude of styles and sizes. It is worth checking whether yours are watertight and adding a lining if not trustworthy. Urns can also have matching plinths (this is more often the case with larger urns).

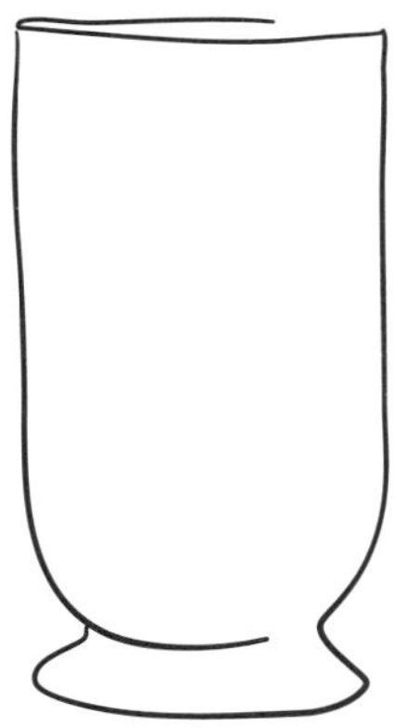
14

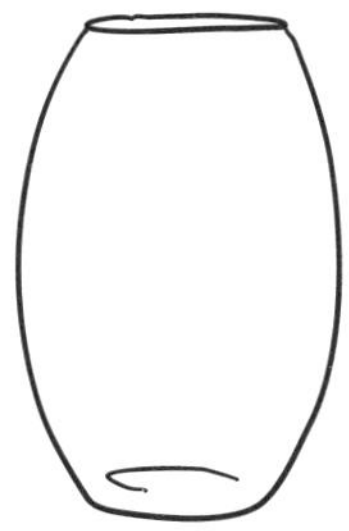
15

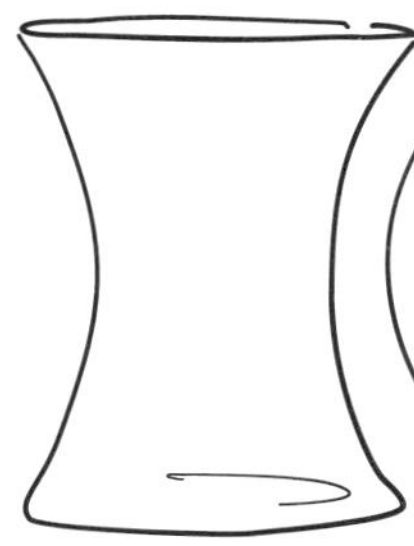
16

17

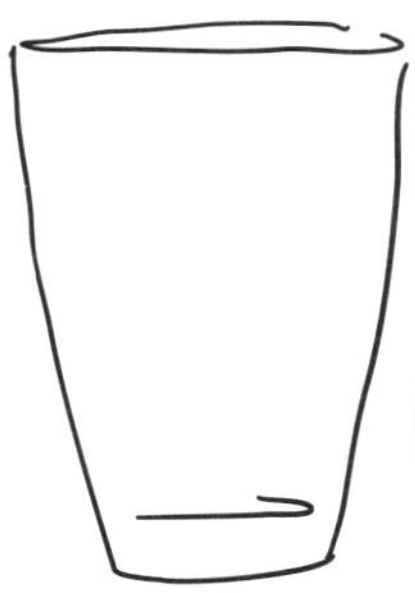
18

19

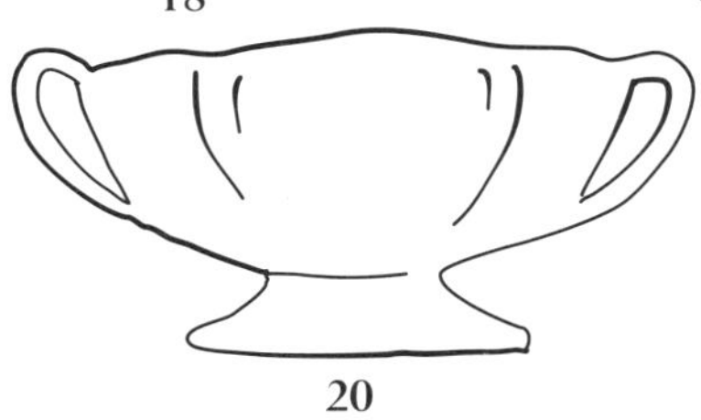
20

21

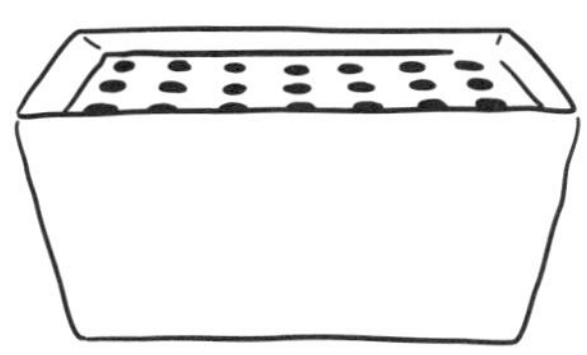
22

23

Cutting

Growth Stage

Most flowers are best picked when they begin to show some colour. If they are picked in full bloom, your flowers will look beautiful but not for long.

The flowers of some plants (such as peonies, roses, and dahlias) may not fully develop if picked in tight bud.

Peony buds will open if picked at the 'marshmallow' stage, when they give a little when pressed between your fingers.

Spire-shaped flowers such as digitalis, verbascum, and gladiolus are best cut when the lowest flowers have opened. The exception to this rule is delphinium spires, which should be cut when most of the flowers have opened, as these may not open further.

Hellebores are stronger and last far longer if picked once a seed pod has formed.
(See fig. 1 on page 15.)

Time of Day

Ideally flowers and foliage should be cut early in the morning when they are fully hydrated.

Cut your flowers when the plants are dry where possible. Cutting in the rain or when the plants are covered in dew can lead to mould forming on flowers and foliage.

Avoid picking flowers or foliage during warm, sunny conditions as plants are at risk of being stressed and the health of your stems is likely be compromised.

If you are not able to pick in the morning, wait until conditions have cooled down, preferably late in the evening. Then the plants will have had a chance to rehydrate.

Always place stems into fresh, clean water immediately after cutting.

Frequency. Generally, annuals such as sweet peas (and some perennials) will bloom for longer if picked regularly.

Picking. Picking is akin to pruning. Pruning heavily can lead to fewer flowers being produced the following season. It is advisable to pick lightly and only occasionally from slower-growing shrubs to avoid distressing the whole plant.

Dried flowers. For flowers that you intend to dry, pick before they are fully open to ensure that the colour lasts and that the petals do not fall off during the drying process.

Tools. Sharp, well-maintained secateurs and scissors ensure good clean cuts without crushing stems and they are easier on the hands too.

Caution! It is good practice to use gloves when picking and handling all cut flowers, particularly those you haven't used before. Parts of some flowers, such as monkshood (Aconitum), are poisonous; others release a milky white sap on cutting which can cause skin irritation.

Avoiding dangerous plants. A guide to potentially harmful plants - The retailers' code of practice for potentially harmful plants (2000) has a useful list of potentially harmful plants in the UK.
See - www.hta.org.uk

Foraging. If you are given foraging rights by landowners, harvest responsibly. Ensure you never take all of whatever you are cutting and be mindful of the ecosystem that you are changing. In the UK it is illegal to gather flowers, moss and foliage from public land for commercial gain (section 4 of the Theft Act 1968). Please do check the laws in your own location.

fig.1

Hellebore stem showing seed pods. Once these pods have begun to form the flowers will last longer when cut.

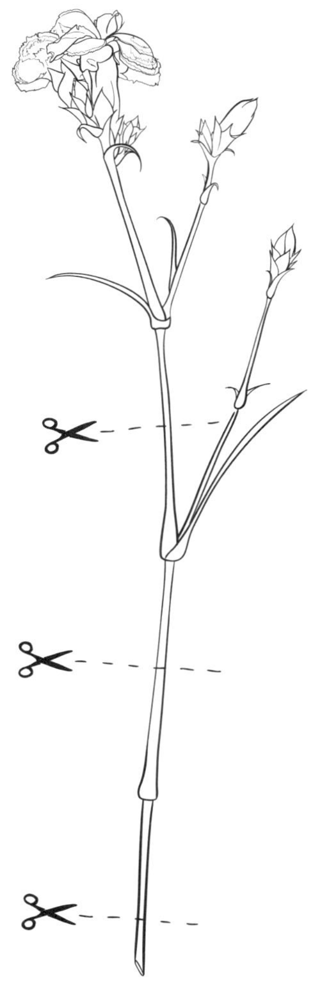

fig.2

Carnation stem. Cut in between the nodes as shown so as not to cause damage and limit water uptake.

Conditioning

Preparing flowers before designing with them is key to ensuring they are strong and hydrated. This applies to all flowers, whether from flower suppliers, from your garden or flower field.

The cleanliness of water and vessels, and proper maintenance of your cutting tools, are essential.

All stems should be cut using a sharp knife, floristry scissors or secateurs, to avoid crushing the stems and reducing their ability to take up water.

Always re-cut stems by at least 1cm. Cut at a sharp angle, to create a greater surface area and allow the stems to drink more easily. Much like using a straw at the bottom of a glass, it is easier to drink if the straw isn't flat to the bottom.

Place stems into cool, fresh water in a clean bucket. Any foliage below the water level should be removed to prevent it from breaking down in the water, which would introduce bacteria and shorten the life of your stems.

To ensure that flowers are fully hydrated before use, leave the stems in a cool, dark place overnight once you have processed them.

Removing thorns from garden rose varieties can shock them into opening quickly, so it's worth waiting as long as possible to ensure they do not open too soon.

Water should be refreshed daily to prevent bacteria from building up.

Some flowers need a little extra processing to remain well hydrated.

Flowers with soft stems and heavy heads, such as tulips and hyacinths, are prone to bending. In order to straighten stems, wrap bunches of the flowers in newspaper and stand them in deep water overnight.

Stems prone to drooping, such as euphorbia, smyrnium, hellebores, and hydrangea, can be sealed by scalding. This means dipping the bottom 2–4cm of the stems into boiling hot water for 10–20 seconds. (Wear gloves when handling euphorbia to protect skin from the milky sap it releases when cut. The sap can cause irritation.) *Drooping roses can also be shocked in this manner* if they remain dehydrated despite being re-cut and placed in clean, cool water.

The stems of *flowers such as tulips, hyacinths, and narcissi are filled with sap* which is released when cut. This sap can have a negative effect on other flowers, so ensure these are not mixed with non-sap filled stems. They should have their ends cut as usual, then be placed into clean water in clean buckets and not mixed with any other stems for at least 4 hours or preferably overnight. After this initial conditioning they can be used alongside other ingredients in mixed designs. Bear in mind, if you re-cut the stems, sap will be released again.

Searing the ends of poppies with a flame for 8–10 seconds can extend their lives by up to a week. If you have a large number to process, a small blow torch can be useful.

Some *flowers such as carnations and pinks* should only be cut in-between their nodes. They are unable to take water up efficiently if cut on the node, or if the node is damaged. (See fig.2 on page 15.)

To help with hydration, *woody stemmed plants such as lilac, viburnum and prunus* can be cut up to 5cm vertically from the base of the stem. Hammering woody stems is no longer recommended as it can introduce bacterial infection and can damage the structure of the stem, leading to less efficient uptake of water.

Flowers with *hollow stems such as delphinium, amaryllis and lupins* can be conditioned by filling the stem with water, plugging the bottom of the stem with cotton wool, then tying a little twine around the base to keep the cotton wool plug in place and to prevent the stem from splitting. If you do not have any cotton wool or prefer not to use cotton, stems can be filled with water as described but then, holding your thumb over the base of the stem to stop water from escaping, you can place the filled stem into a bucket of deep water, releasing your finger once the stem bottom is under the water.

Alongside its need for a little assistance with hydration, *amaryllis has large, top-heavy blooms and benefits from being supported.* A cane can be inserted inside the hollow stems to minimise the chance of bending and breaking. To support these delicate, oversized blooms as they open, place them into a grid in a bucket as outlined on pages 22–23.

Dahlias can be a little temperamental. They do not travel particularly well or last very long but they can be encouraged to last longer if given flower food and put into warm water.

There are some stems that will turn the water dirty overnight even if you have clean buckets and water, and sharply cut stems. Flowers such as *chrysanthemums and zinnias and foliage such as rosemary or senecio will make the water look dirty* very quickly. This can be resolved by adding a dash of weak sterilising solution to ensure clear, clean water in your vases.

Methods

We include some notes on general floristry here, alongside some methods of working that you might find useful.

Sourcing

Supporting local growers can take a little more effort and energy than ordering from a single, larger wholesaler but it brings with it many rewards. Using seasonal flowers and foliage reduces the carbon footprint of the industry, while offering interesting and often unexpected choice. For example, flowers and foliage that do not normally travel well over long distances become options for your floral palette. The scent of flowers and foliage is also notable in locally grown flowers, something which is otherwise often bred out in favour of straight stems and a generally more consistent product. By using local suppliers, we can vouch for the welfare of the growers, pickers, and the packers of the stems that we use, as well as the chemicals they have been processed with.

Rules on foraging will differ depending on where you are, so please seek local advice before cutting flowers or foliage on any land that does not belong to you. The Theft Act 1968, for England and Wales, states that:

"A person who picks mushrooms growing wild on any land, or who picks flowers, fruit or foliage from a plant growing wild on any land, does not (although not in possession of the land) steal what he picks, unless he does it for reward or for sale or other commercial purpose."

At the time of writing there is a common law right in England and Wales to forage for 'the four 'f's' (flowers, fruit, foliage and fungi as long as it's for your own personal use and the plant is growing wild). Collecting wild food or picking cultivated crops for commercial gain is theft.

Practical notes on creating designs

Working in a considered and sustainable manner isn't restricted to wild and loose styles. *Any* style can be achieved with a little consideration, suitable mechanics, and the right flowers.

When creating floral designs, preparation is key. Any combination of flowers and foliage can be used. Some floral designs such as buttonholes and flower crowns require flowers and foliage to hold well out of water. If you are unfamiliar with the longevity of a flower or foliage, experiment with materials ahead of designing to ensure that you have elements that are appropriate.

In order to test the longevity of flowers and foliage stems with which we are unfamiliar, we suspend them from a line. In the Floribunda Rose Studio, this is known as the Washing Line of Doom. We check to see how stems are looking after one hour, two hours, a few hours, and the next day. Those that stay well hydrated out of water for 24 hours are deemed resilient enough to be used for floral designs that could not easily be given a water source.

Flowers and foliage must be well conditioned before use. (See pages 16–17 on conditioning.) Ensure that your buckets are clean, your tools are in good working order, and that you have a clean, ideally cool, space to work in. It is worth checking that you have all of the tools, equipment and sundries required before beginning to work.

Take a little time to lay your conditioned ingredients out on your workbench ahead of creating designs such as hand-tied bouquets, buttonholes or any other designs which you will be holding in your hand as you make them. This enables you to see and get access to your stems easily. You're likely to only have one hand free while making these arrangements.

Flowering foliage can be useful in some situations as it gives you a bit of a head start. This is akin to adding filler flowers alongside your foliage which can save you time. Home-grown flowering foliage is as valuable as the flowers themselves; each kind reflects a short window of time. For example, scented lilac will only flower for a few short weeks.

Fragrance is something we're always looking to incorporate into our work, it has strong links to memory. We use fragrance wherever possible – to add layers of meaning and memory to designs. Even in the depths of winter there is fragrance to be found if you search hard enough.

Taping stems

We tape a lot of stems with waxed floral tape to keep them from losing water in installations, these are then taped or wired onto pieces of foliage or into chicken wire.

We use waxed floral tape; a biodegradable tape made of crepe paper covered in a soft wax. It is not sticky until the warmth of your hands has softened the wax. It must be pulled and kept taut in order to expose the wax.

If you pull too tightly it will snap. If this does happen, you can simply add another piece. The more familiar you become with the technique the easier it becomes to gauge how tightly to pull. If you don't pull it taut, the tape can unravel, as it won't have stuck properly. It is better to pull too tightly than not tightly enough.

Start at the top of the wire or stem and take your taut tape around the stem (or wire) once or twice. Then pressing the tape to the stem or wire, carry on down the stem or wire with the tape at an angle, ensuring that there are no gaps. Overlapping is absolutely fine. Continue until you get to the end of the section that you want to tape. Then, come back on yourself a little. If you are taping just the end of a stem, start around 4cm from the end then tape down to the end, covering the entire end of the stem with tape. (You may need to go around a few times.) Finally, tape back up the stem to ensure that it is secure and completely sealed.

Wiring

Stub wires come in different lengths, finishes, colours and gauges. The gauge is indicated by the number, the higher the number the finer the wire. Lower gauges are the most robust and can be used when the maximum strength and support is required. We rarely wire flowers or foliage elements but do use wires for the base of flower crowns. Heavier gauge wires are best for this.

When wiring flowers, the wire is either used to support the stem or the stem is cut off and the wire is used in place of the stem. Waxed florist tape is used to cover the wire either way. It is advisable to use the finest gauge wire possible to avoid wired flowers looking stiff and unnatural.

Vessels

Often overlooked in floral design, vessels are hugely important. A carefully considered choice of vessel can elevate a design. Any vessel can become the basis for a floral design. Pages 10–13 outline the more common vessels found and a little about their uses.

Designing into sustainable mechanics

When designing into mechanics; typically, we suggest starting with branches or larger elements (these are often referred to as the leading lines of a design. It is easier to achieve the overall shape of the design that you are aiming for if you begin with a framework of a shape before adding in the rest of your foliage. As you add stems, your design will begin to feel more secure as the stems begin to create a network. Next, flowers. Add focal, then filler flowers. Delicate and trailing elements are generally added last.

We try to avoid single-use plastics where possible, favouring mechanics which are reusable. This book does not include instructions for the use of floral foam as it is a single-use plastic that we can work without.

Initially, working in chicken wire can feel different from working in floral foam. Where foam is solid, wire is forgiving. In wire, should you wish to, you have the option to insert stems and then to change your mind without ruining the mechanics or limiting your options.

It's worth noting that it will be easier to remove stems and re-position them if they're cleared of any lumps or bumps ahead of use (otherwise they may get caught in the wire). That said, for added stability in larger designs, those lumps and bumps getting caught in the wire can be of use as they will become anchored more effectively.

In place of cable ties, we have found that hook-and-loop strapping (most commonly known as Velcro) can be used. It is incredibly strong and is used for securing and attaching a range of things in a number of designs throughout the book.

'Sausages', 'mossages' and 'fossages'

We have developed many techniques that don't rely on single-use plastics over the years, three of these floral mechanics have been tested, trialled and used in numerous ways. We refer to them in the studio as 'sausages', 'mossages' and 'fossages'.

The chicken wire *'sausage'* is a piece of chicken wire (of any length) rolled into a cylinder and joined together using the ends of the wire. Sausages became the base of the armatures we use for wide, oversized bouquets (see page 46), floral clouds (see page 84), and other installations.

Then came the *'mossage'* which was made in the same way but this time filled with damp moss. The mossage was not useful for larger installations as it was too heavy, messy, and was prone to leaking. In all honesty it was not good enough. Moss based designs come into their own for wreaths, funeral crosses, and coffin toppers though. We soon realised that we could make these completely biodegradable by using string rather than wire.

The *'fossage'* is a cylinder of chicken wire filled with foliage. After using the 'sausage' for some time, we found it lacked sufficient grip to support the stems we were adding, so we added foliage inside the cylinder to give stems better hold. This made the new version far more viable. It is light, easy to transport and proved less messy than the 'mossage'. Filled with foliage instead of moss, it became known as a 'fossage' in the studio.

Though the 'fossage' doesn't hold water, means of hydration such as tubes can be added easily and don't fall through thanks to the foliage inside the chicken wire cylinder. The 'fossage' features in flower filled arches on page 78 and can also be used in larger free-form installations.

Once you have created your design

It can be useful to take photographs of any floral designs, during the creating process and on completion. These photos not only record what you have made but can show any gaps or areas that might need a little further attention. This can be useful for overview, particularly if there is no one around for a second opinion.

If transporting arrangements to another site, a kit bag is invaluable. For recommended contents, see the 'Working Off Site' section on page 94.

It is good practice to change the water and re-cut the base of all stems regularly (every other day, ideally), cutting the stem at least 1cm each time.

In order to refresh the water in an arrangement that cannot be easily removed from the vessel, take the arrangement to a tap and run cool water gently into the dish, allowing the water to overflow from the vessel. If your design is too large to be refreshed under a tap indoors, either take the arrangement to a tap outside or take it outside and use a watering can to refresh the water in the same manner.

Remove any dead or dying materials to keep the arrangement looking fresher for longer.

Where possible, position your design in a cool spot away from direct sources of heat such as radiators and fires.

Keep flowers away from fruit bowls. As fruits ripen, they release ethylene, which ages flowers prematurely.

Keep in mind the fact that any tulips used in your design will continue to grow. They are also phototropic and will bend towards the light, unless you rotate your design a little each day.

Waste

It is possible to work with flowers and create little waste. Many local flower growers pack their flowers in paper wraps rather than plastic, some use natural twine instead of plastic twine or elastic bands for bundling them together, but that is not always the case.

There are still many suppliers of home-grown and imported flowers and foliage who send their produce to market in plastic. This plastic packaging can be used as padding for transporting floral designs, sent back to the supplier, or disposed of. Used bubble wrap is also useful for packing designs before transport. We re-use it many times, particularly as padding in between bottles of flowers or around glass and ceramic vessels. Cardboard flower boxes can be reused or recycled.

If you have local growers, it is common practice to collect flowers in your own buckets.

Green waste that is generated can be composted if you have the space and equipment. A woodchipper can be used to break down large branches before they are composted, as can smaller stems. A huge amount of green waste can be broken down into a surprisingly small volume that way.

Deliveries and working off site

Flowers can be delivered to clients in water, using recycled (where possible) glass vessels which themselves can be reused or recycled.

If installing floral designs off site, a bucket of additional flowers and foliage allows you the option of replacing any stems ahead of an event.

Some venues dislike the idea of floral designs in vessels which hold water on account of the potential for water damage to historic floors and furniture. In situations like those, adding some sustainably sourced moss inside the vessels minimises the risk of spillage by reducing the movement of water in the vessel.

Insurance

While insurance might not be a legal requirement, it is heavily advised that if you are trading, you make sure that you, your workforce and the general public are safe, and that your business is legally covered should the unexpected happen.

The insurance you need will depend on your circumstances and the legal requirements of the country you are in. Public liability insurance, employers' liability insurance and business interruption insurance are strongly recommended.

Grids

This technique can be the basis for designs or a useful way to support delicate blooms with large delicate heads while they are stored ahead of use. If you are using a small vessel for standard-sized stems, a piece of tape every 2cm should be sufficient.

The technique can be scaled up and used for large stemmed flowers such as amaryllis that have delicate top-heavy heads which need to be protected from bruising. If using a large bucket to hold stems such as amaryllis, tape every 6cm, ensuring that your tape overlaps the vessel by at least 6cm.

Tools

- Scissors

Equipment & Sundries

- Watertight or lined vessel of your choice
- Water jug
- Tape (clear pot tape is ideal for glass vessels or paper tape is a biodegradable option)

1. Make sure that your vessel is clean and dry. The easiest-shaped vessel to start creating grids with is a square or rectangular vase with straight walls, but any stable watertight or lined vessel can be used. Measure the opening of your vessel.

2. Initially, add pieces of tape from the left to the right of the opening of the vessel ensuring that the tape is at least 2cm over the edge of the vessel on either side, to be certain that it holds firmly

3. Next turn the vessel 90° and create the rest of the grid in the same way.

4. Add water to your vase, doing so carefully if using paper tape because paper tape becomes weaker if allowed to get very wet.

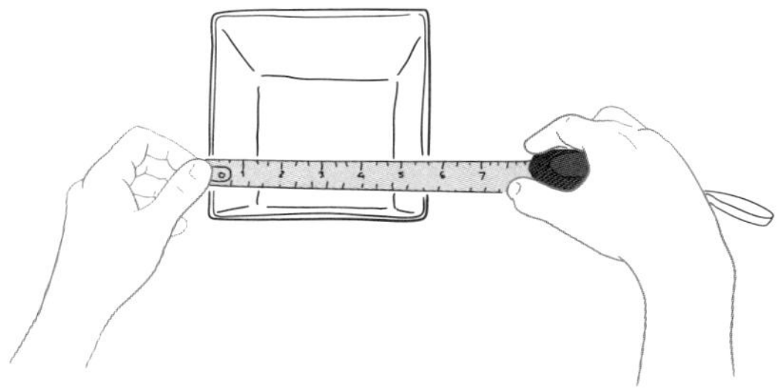

1

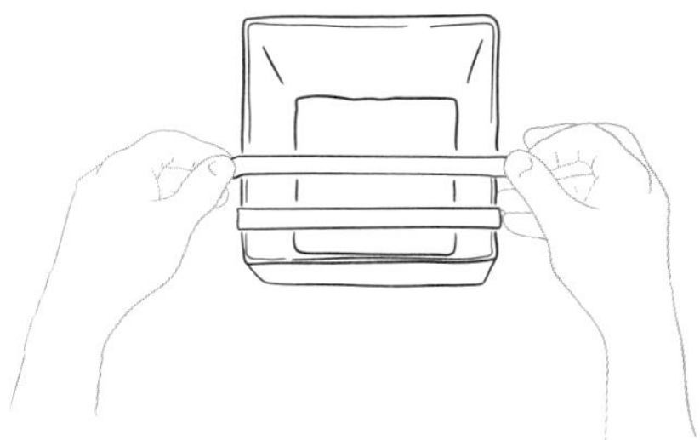

2

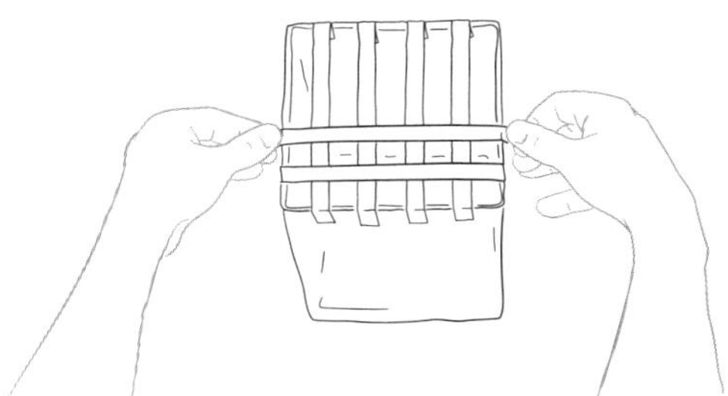

3

4

Kenzan (Pin Holders)

Kenzan come in many shapes and sizes and are available in a variety of materials.

Once you have chosen a vessel for your floral design, select a kenzan which fits easily in the base. Kenzan can be used without fixing to the vessel, but it is a good idea to secure your kenzan so that your floral design is stable. Museum wax or floral fix can be used to do this.

Tools

- Floristry scissors

Equipment & Sundries

- Kenzan
- Museum wax/ Fix/Tac

1. To prepare stems for designing into kenzan, stems should be cut straight rather than at an angle.
2. Take a small section of the wax or fix and roll into a ball. The warmth of your hands will make it more malleable.
3. Once it is soft and easy to mould, press the ball of museum wax/floral fix gently into the base of your vessel, keeping it in place. Typically, the ball of wax/fix will be a little smaller than the base of the kenzan.
4. Press the kenzan down onto the wax/fix to secure it, leaving it to harden for a few minutes before adding water to your vessel and then arranging your stems. Museum wax should ideally be left to set for 12 hours after the kenzan has been pressed onto it, so it is worth preparing these ahead of use. The fix should cover most of the surface area underneath the kenzan once it has been pressed down.

The pins in a kenzan will support the stems of flowers and foliage. Your stems do not need to be placed vertically, they can be inserted between the pins, onto the pins, and at any angle, so long as the base of your stem remains under the water. Kenzan can be covered with moss, pebbles, stones or beads should you wish to disguise them.

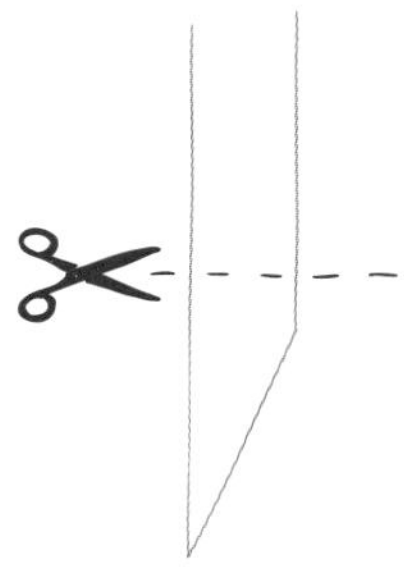

1

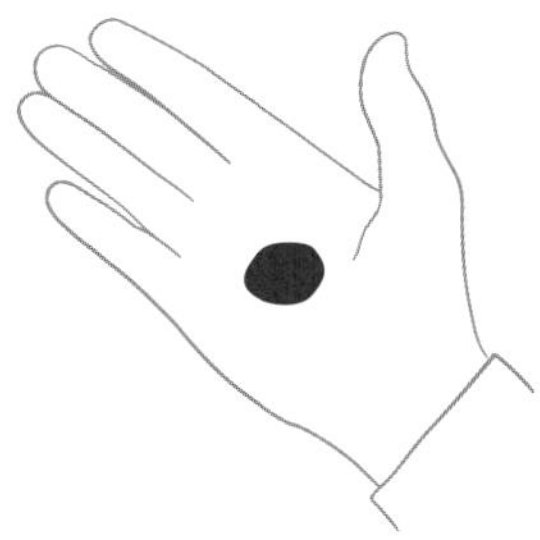

2

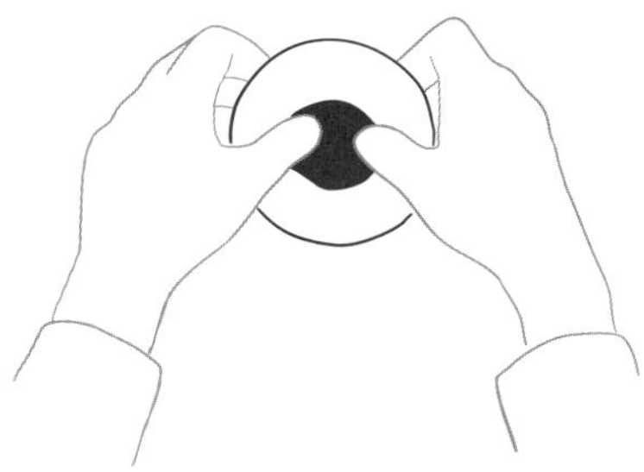

3

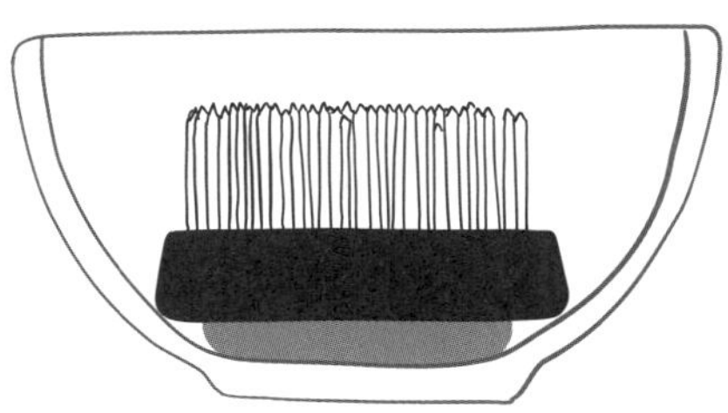

4

Kokedama

When you are choosing plants for kokedama, for kokedama that will be hung indoors, plants such as orchids and asparagus ferns work well. It is advisable to work on an oil cloth or a table that can be wiped down easily as moss can be messy to work with.

If you are planning to hang your kokedama indoors, be sure to choose a house plant which is suited to the conditions of the space that you have in mind. Outdoors, plants can be used for kokedama and then replanted in pots or in the ground when they have finished flowering (or if you want to change the display). Kokedama can also be added to funeral work, hanging installations, arches and wreaths.

Tools

- Fabric scissors
- Floristry scissors

Equipment & Sundries

- Multipurpose, peat-free compost
- Bonsai compost
- Moss
- A plant of your choice
- Twine
- Water spray

1. Soak your plant for 24 hours ahead of beginning the Kokedama process, then remove the plant and carefully tease any excess soil from the roots.

2. Mix equal parts of bonsai compost with multipurpose compost and enough water to create a thick, wet mixture. Add this generously around the roots and shape to form a ball. Plants of different sizes will need different amounts of soil, ensure that you have added plenty as this will nourish the plant and allow room for growth.

3. Lay a sheet of grass moss on to your workbench, larger sections make the process simpler. Position your plant onto the moss ensuring the top edge of the moss reaches the base of the plant. Next, wrap the moss carefully and generously around the base of your plant. Should you find that there is not enough moss to cover the root ball fully, add more as required. The plant should be generously covered. (Having a second person to help hold the plant/moss can be useful at this stage, particularly for larger plants.)

4. Cut a piece of twine at least 3m in length. If using a large plant, you may need more twine. Start with the centre of the twine at the back of the root ball. Use the twine to secure the moss to the root ball by pulling the twine tightly to the front. Be careful to avoid damaging the top of your plant while securing moss to the root ball. Twist or knot the twine at the front, then take it around again in the same way until all of the moss has been secured to the root ball. When you are satisfied that the moss is securely held in place, tie off with a double knot. Tie off the first length and add another until you are confident that all moss is held firmly.

5. Take a length of twine twice the length of the height of the place from which you wish to suspend your kokedama. Double it over and knot the ends to create a loop. Feed the knotted end underneath a point near the top of your kokedama where your twine crosses over. Pull the knot through the string to create a loop that you can suspend your plant from.

Give the moss a trim for a more even finish if required.

See overleaf for how to care for Kokedama.

1

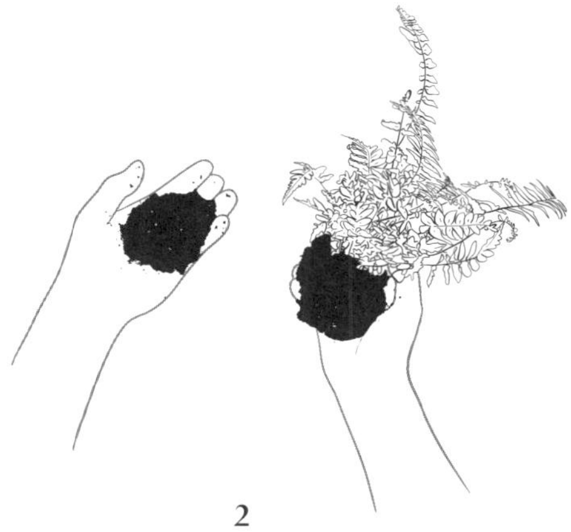

2

3

4

5

Caring for kokedama

Keep your kokedama out of direct sunlight to avoid the moss from being damaged and to stop the root ball from drying out.

Spray daily with water. If the root ball feels light, place your kokedama into a bucket or a bowl of water and allow it to soak for a few minutes. Let it drain briefly and then re-hang. The amount of water that your plants need will depend on your plant choice and the climate that you are in.

Use a weak dilution of seaweed or suitable plant food in the bucket of water that you soak your moss ball in.

To re-pot, remove the moss, add more soil and then re-moss, before hanging up again. Do this once or twice a year depending on how much your plant has been growing.

Bowl Arrangements

Tools

- Wire cutters
- Leather gardening gloves (if desired)

Equipment & Sundries

- Watertight or lined vessel
- Chicken wire
- Pot tape
- Turntable (if desired)

1. To work out the size of your chicken wire (both length and width) measure the width of the top of your vessel, then double it. You should end up with a square.
2. Cut the chicken wire to size.
3. Bring the corners towards the middle of the square to create a ball.
4. Tuck the ends of the chicken wire inward.
5. Check that the ball is an even shape. Ensure that there are no ends sticking out.
6. Your chicken wire ball should now fit the vessel. Place it with the rounded top facing up so that it's sitting just proud of the top of your chosen vessel with the edges facing downward.
7. Using pot tape, secure the chicken wire in a cross shape. Once it is secured, pinch the sticky sides of the tape together. This avoids the tape sticking to stems later.
8. Top up your vessel with water. Ahead of transportation, empty a little water. This prevents water loss while in transit. Ensure that all vessels are adequately refilled once in situ.

Arrange flowers and foliage into the prepared vessel ensuring that the chicken wire is not visible. A turntable is invaluable for creating these designs. Turning the turntable rather than the design or having to walk around the workbench allows for greater overview. The first few stems may seem a little unstable, but once there is a network of stems in place the whole design will feel secure.

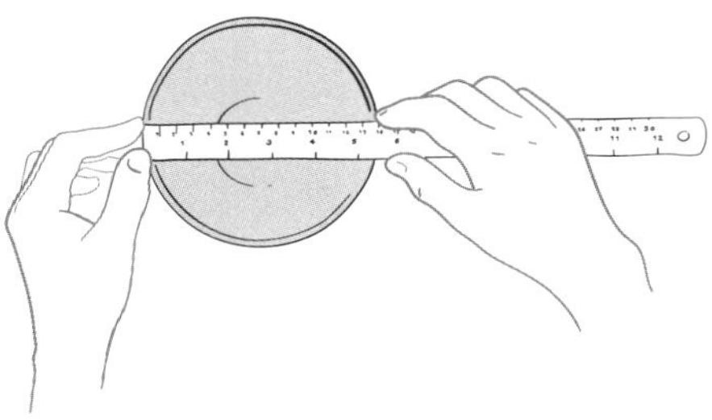

1

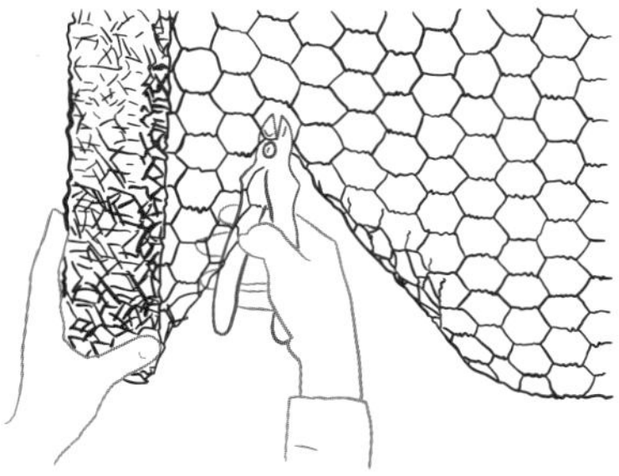

2

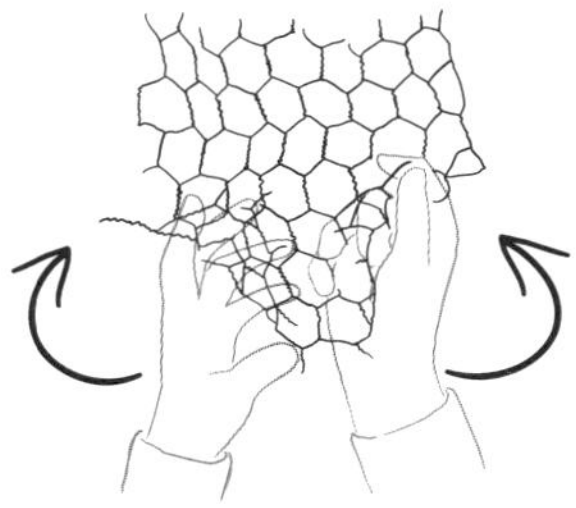

3

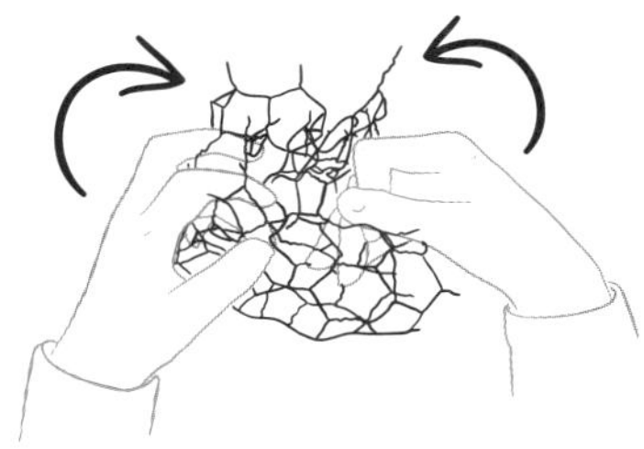

4

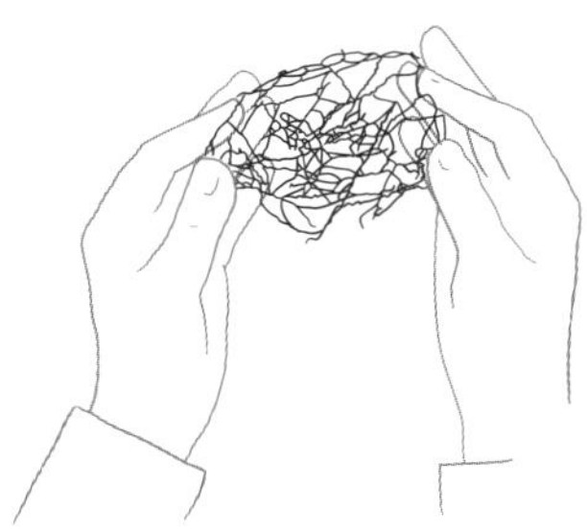

5

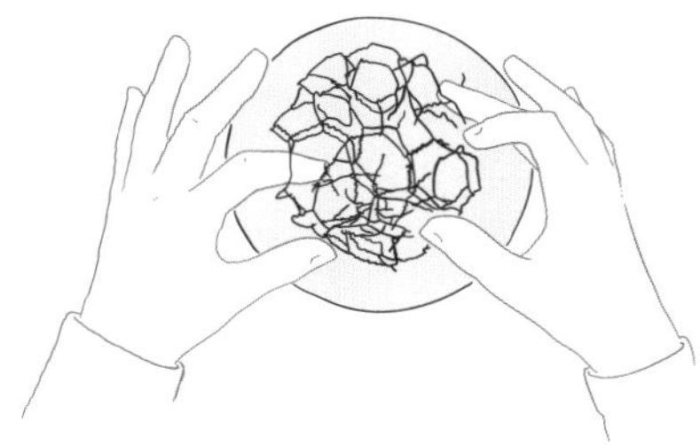

6

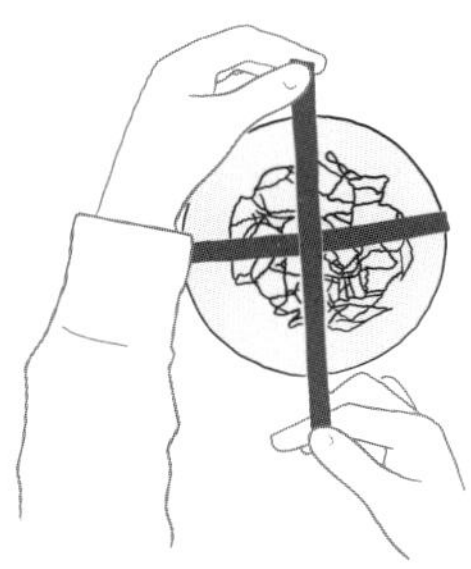

7

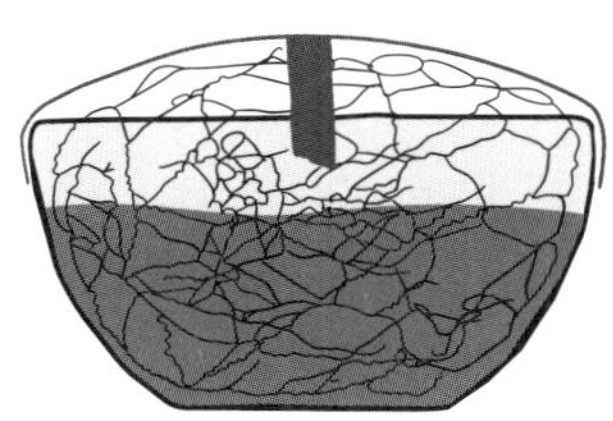

8

High Table Centre Arrangements

High table arrangements are made in the same manner as bowl arrangements, though in this case wide, shallow vessels are used for stability which can be placed onto stands or vases for height.

Tools

- Floristry scissors
- Wire cutters
- Leather gardening gloves (if desired)

Equipment & Sundries

- Low dish
- Chicken wire
- Turntable
- Round bucket
- Pot tape
- Stand

1. To work out the size of your chicken wire (both length and width) measure the width of the top of your vessel, then double it. You should end up with a square.
2. Cut the chicken wire to size.
3. Bring the corners towards the middle of the square to create a ball.
4. Tuck the ends of the chicken wire inward.
5. Check that the ball is an even shape. Ensure that there are no ends sticking out.
6. Your chicken wire ball should now fit the vessel. Have it rounded top facing up so that it's sitting just proud of the top of your chosen vessel with the edges facing downward.

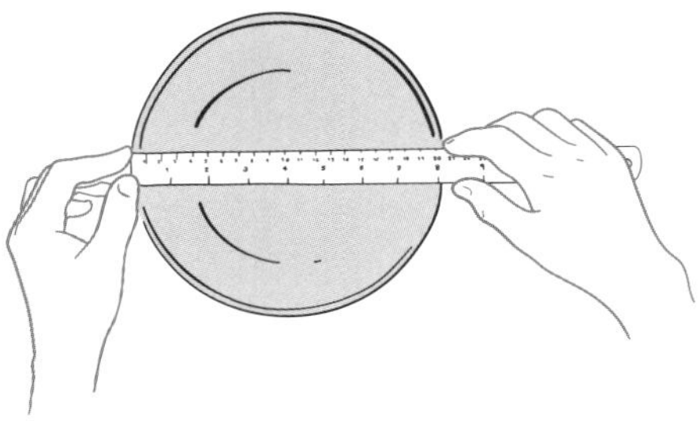

1

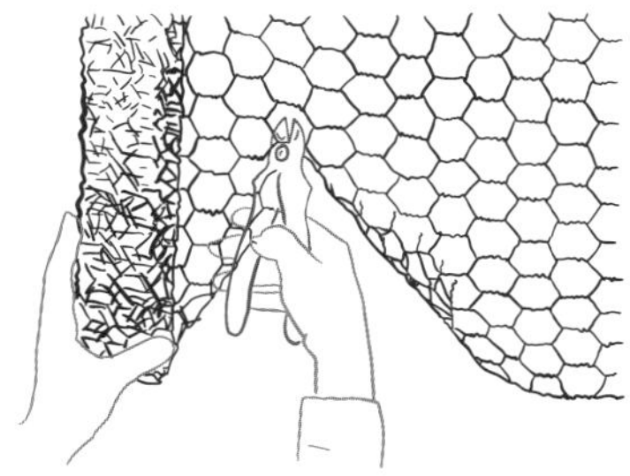

2

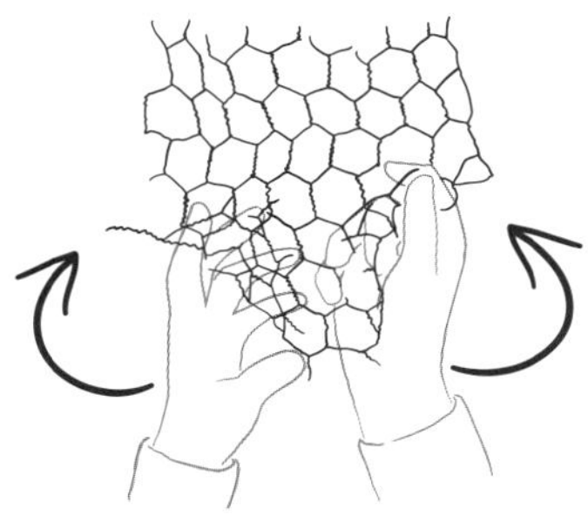

3

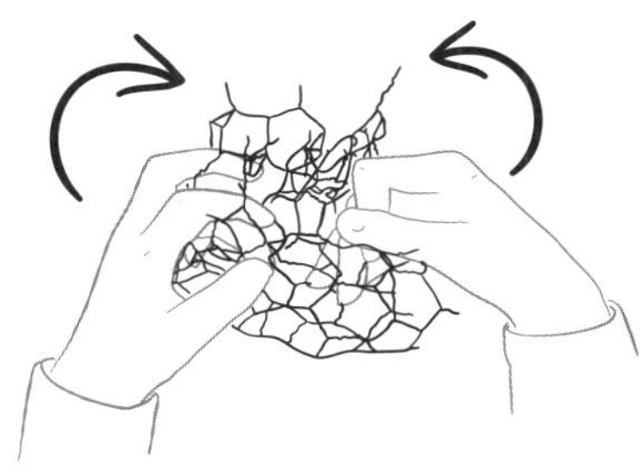

4

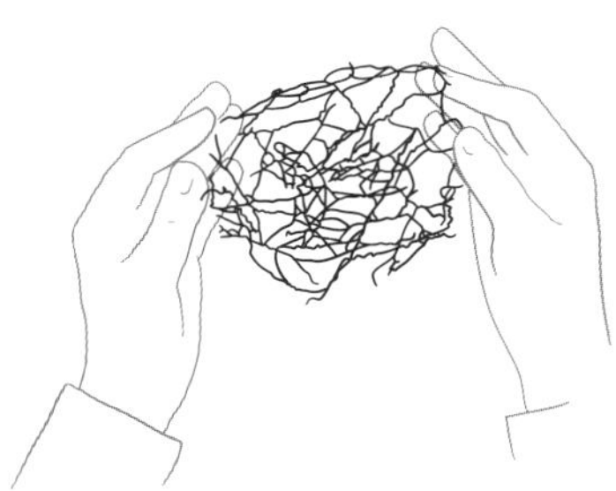

5

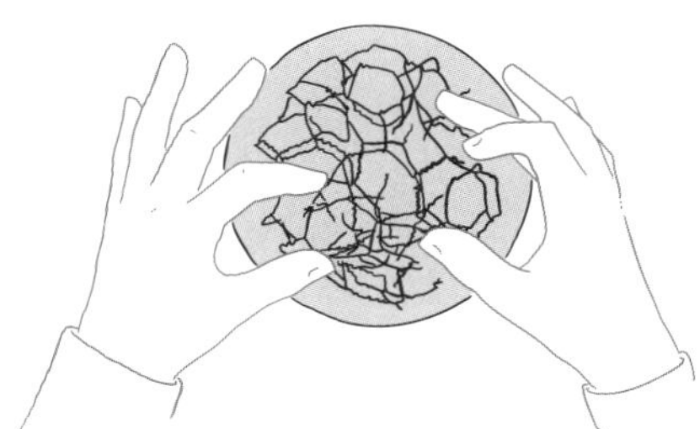

6

High Table Centre Arrangements (continued)

7. Using pot tape, secure the chicken wire in a cross shape. Once it is secured, pinch the sticky sides of the tape together. This avoids the tape sticking to stems later.

8. Make sure that your vessel is full of water. Arrange your flowers and foliage into your prepared vessel.

9. Once on site, place your stands in position and add the tall table arrangement onto your elevated stand. Top up with water if necessary. Check it over, and then add trailing elements which will hide the vessel from view.

Placing your vessel on top of an upturned bucket on a turntable makes creating designs with trailing elements easier. You can add stems and turn as you go meaning that you won't have to keep walking around your vessel. The first few stems may seem a little unstable if you aren't familiar with working in chicken wire, but once you have a network of stems in place your whole design will feel more secure.

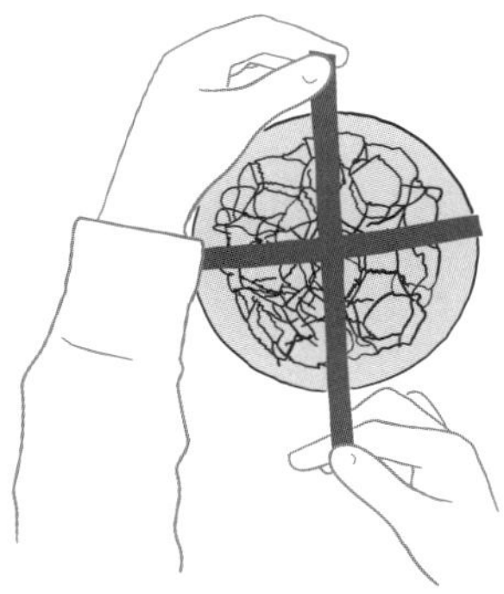

7

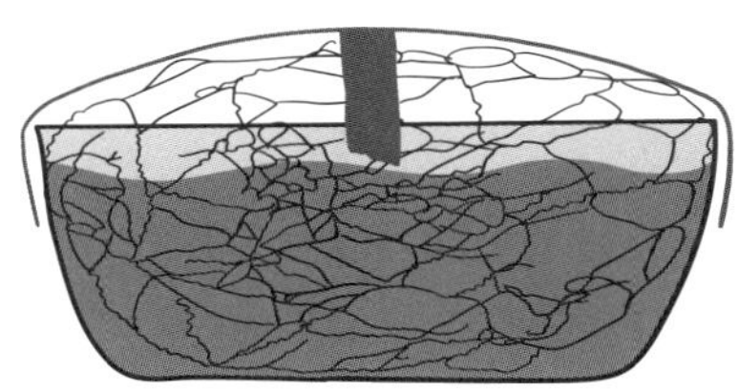

8

9

Buttonholes and Corsages

Tools

- Floristry scissors
- Fabric scissors, if cutting ribbons

Equipment & Sundries

- A bowl or water glass
- Waxed floral tape
- Ribbon/twine
- Pins

1. Lay out your well-conditioned ingredients, ensuring that each of the elements that you have chosen lasts well out of water. Very delicate stems can be wired with fine wires and taped individually if needed.

2. Gather your chosen flowers and foliage stems between your thumb and forefinger ensuring there are no leaves below the point at which you are holding them.

3. At this point, small adjustments can be made if needed by gently pulling stems up or down until you are happy with the design.

4. Tape your elements together with waxed floral tape, ensuring that you have pulled it tightly so that it sticks to itself. Trim the ends for a tidy finish. If you are making buttonholes ahead of the day they will be needed, leave the stems a little longer and cut them neatly on the morning of the event so that they look their best.

5. Finish your buttonholes or corsages with twine or ribbon (there are a multitude of options) to hide the tape.

6. Place into a bowl of water for up to 48 hours until needed. Your designs will stay fresh by drinking through the petals, leaves and stems.

Buttonholes are worn on the left lapel of a suit and are often worn by the men in a wedding party: the groom, best man, ushers, father of the bride, father of the groom and any page boys.

Corsages are made in exactly the same way as buttonholes. Typically these have more floral elements included and they tend to be a little larger in size. Traditionally they are worn with the flowers facing down on the right lapel of a jacket by the mothers of the bride and the groom, though these days most people prefer the flowers upward.

Rosemary will turn black if submerged, so if including this herb in your buttonholes or corsages, place the finished item into small water glasses or tea light holders rather than a bowl so that it drinks through the stem without discolouring until it is needed. Ensure that the leaves are not submerged.

Before submerging any flower or foliage in water, test its suitability by trialling a single stem for 48 hours.

1

2

3

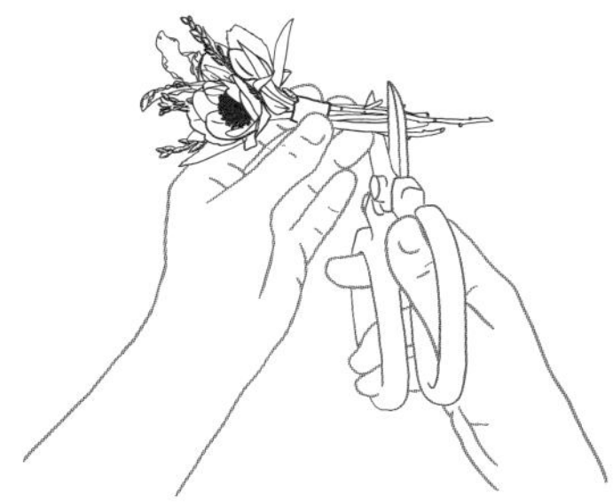

4

5

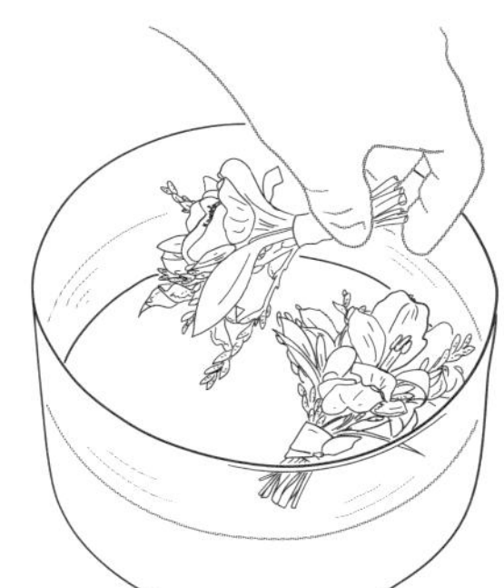

6

Flower Crowns

Flower crowns are typically made using stub wires covered with waxed florists tape as a base, but can also be created on a length of willow, or other strong flexible natural materials such as lengths of ivy twisted together and joined at the ends - the important thing is that you have a supportive flexible and preferably lightweight base. If you are making a crown based on anything other than stub wires, tape your base to help stems to stay in place and begin at step 5.

Tools

- Floristry Scissors

Equipment & Sundries

- A wide bowl or bucket of water
- Floristry tape
- Ribbon/Twine
- 18-20 gauge stub wires
- Flowers
- Foliage
- Textural elements such as seed pods, grasses as per your design

1. Tape two 18–20 gauge stub wires from start to finish.
2. Choose whether you want to create a flower crown that is finished with loops for ribbons or one that is finished with a loop and hook to create a continuous circle. Finishing with ribbons is recommended if you do not have exact head measurements as this is the more adjustable option. Depending on which finishing method you intend to use, take your two taped stub wires and twist the ends into either two loops, or a hook and a loop as shown.
3. Measure out your required length. This will be the circumference of the head of the intended wearer.
4. Twist the wires together to create one wire, ensuring that you still have the length that you need.
5. Tape over the joined section making sure that it if feels stable. If it's not feeling completely stable you can go over it again, being certain that you are pulling the tape tightly enough to stick it securely to itself.
6. Cut your well-conditioned florals and selection of foliage to size and lay out on your workbench.
7. To start adding fresh ingredients, first tape a tapered piece of foliage onto the wire using florist's tape. Ensure that you have sealed the stem end with tape
8. Bend your crown before you add further flowers and foliage. This makes for more even coverage when the crown is worn.

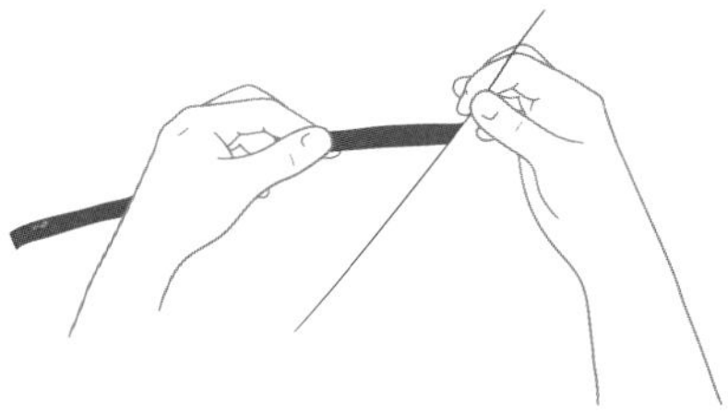

1

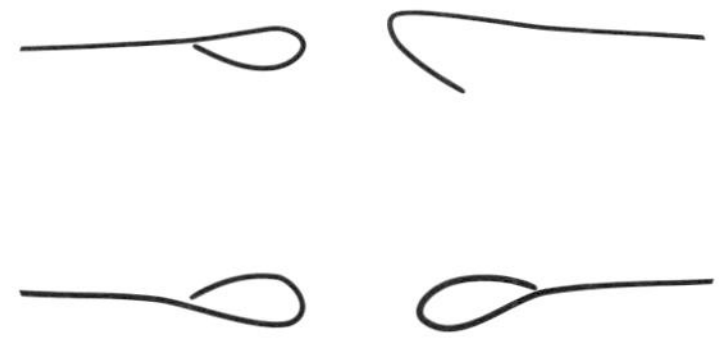

2

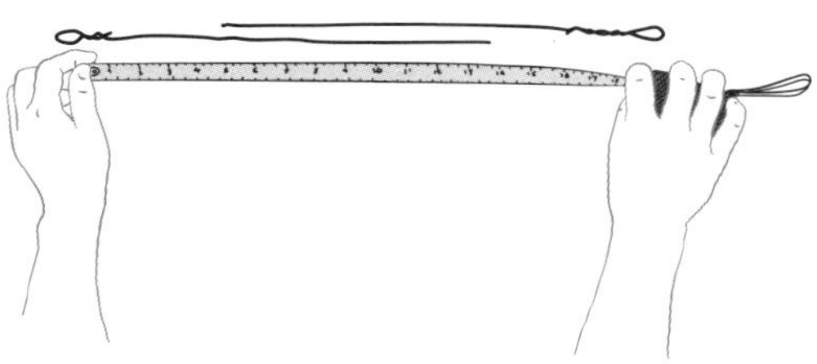

3

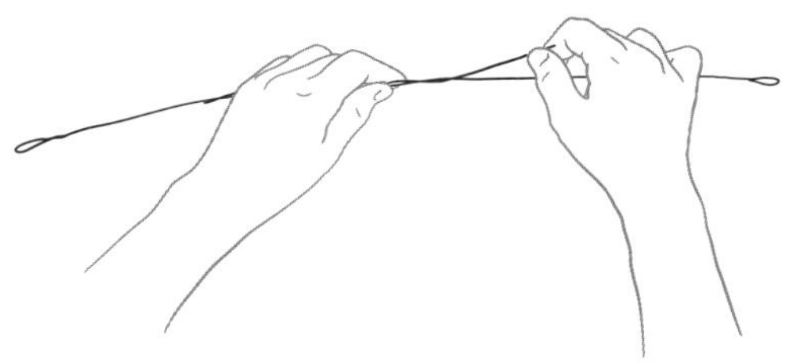

4

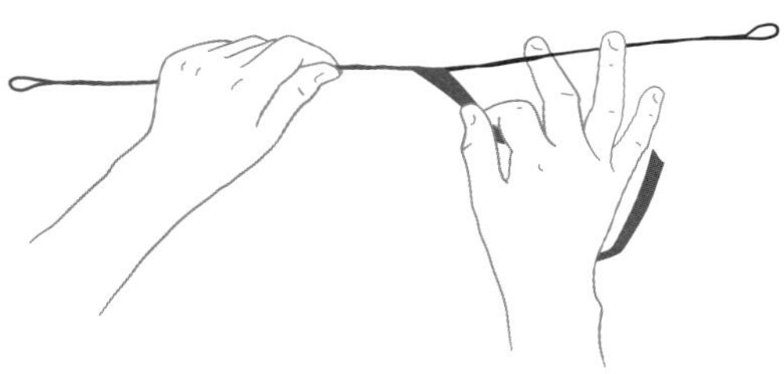

5

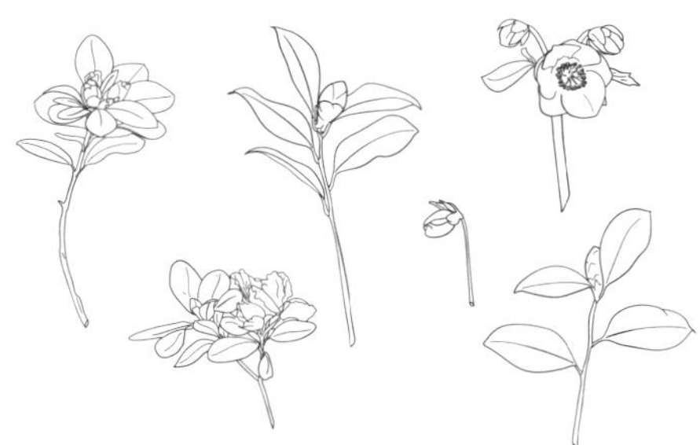

6

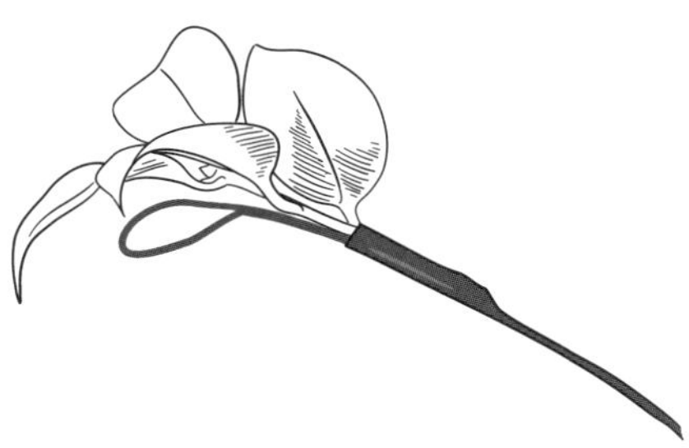

7

8

Flower Crowns (continued)

9. Place the stems of each element in the same direction as you build up your design. Moving along the taped wire a little each time you add flowers or foliage pieces, angling new stems to the left, along the middle and to the right, for full coverage. Each new flower or piece of foliage should overlap the taped stems of the previous elements. Ensure that every stem is taped to the crown.

For a continuous flower crown with a hook and a loop

10a. For flower crowns that are finished with a hook at one end and a loop on the other, simply put the hook through loop and you will have a continuous circle thanks to the tapered end that you started with.

For a flower crown with ribbons

10b. If creating the crown with two loop ends, you will need to finish with a piece of taped foliage or a taped flower in the opposite direction to that in which your other elements were all positioned. This single piece can be taped on, or wired on to a piece of existing foliage or on to your frame, if that's easier.

11. Finish your flower crown with twine or ribbon, leaving the ends long enough for tying into a bow or knot with trails according to your design.

When complete:

Place your finished flower crown into a bowl of water for up to 48 hours until it is needed. The flowers and foliage on your crown will drink through their petals, leaves and stems.

Between 30 minutes to an hour before needed, remove your crown from the water and place onto a towel or tea towel to allow petals to dry. Silk ribbons will dry in a matter of seconds if gently patted dry with a tea towel.

NB - Rosemary will turn black if submerged so is not a good choice for crowns you wish to make in advance.

If using a mixture of dried and fresh ingredients, do not submerge it but make it shortly before the time required.

9

10a

10b

11

Hand-Tied Bouquets

When making hand-tied bouquets, you will be holding stems in one hand and adding with the other. Before beginning to make your bouquet, decide which hand you will be holding the bouquet with (generally your non-dominant hand), and which hand will be free to add flowers.

Tools

- Floristry scissors
- Fabric Scissors

Equipment & Sundries

- Twine
- Flowers
- Foliage
- Ribbon
- Vase or Bucket

1. Lay out your well-conditioned ingredients on your workbench; it is useful to have all elements within reach before beginning.
2. Start by placing one stem in the hand you will be holding the bouquet in. Then, selecting another stem with your other hand, cross it over the stem you're already holding. The stems will rest in the palm of your holding hand, held by your thumb and forefinger.
3. At every third element (approximately) turn the bunch about a quarter turn in your holding hand and continue adding flowers and foliage. Ensure that you add all stems in the same direction and turn your bunch the same way every time. The stems will begin to form a spiral so long as you continue to add each element in the same direction as the last.
4. Continue adding flowers and foliage, turning the bunch about a quarter turn every three (or so) additions, always in the same direction.
5. If a more rounded shape is desired, place each layer of flowers and foliage a little further down from the previous layer until you are happy with your design.

1

2

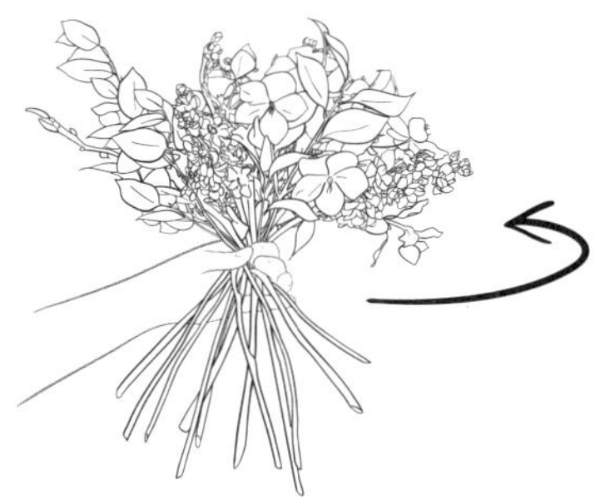

3

4

5

Hand-Tied Bouquets (continued)

6. Complete the design with foliage stems for a tidy finish as well as for protection of the softer or more delicate stems.
7. Then, holding the end of your string with the little finger of your non-dominant hand, wrap the string/twine around the stems so that they're firmly held in place.
8. Tie off with a double knot at the tie point. (The tie point is the narrowest point of the bouquet, where you have been holding it.) Cut the twine for a neat finish.
9. Cut your stems to one length. Holding the stems together will make this easier.

Hand-tied bouquets or posies can be used in all manner of vessels and are ideal for simple table centres. Stems should reach the bottom of the vessel, unless it's to be a bouquet that will be carried, in which case the stems can be cut shorter.

Large bouquets with longer stems can be used in tall vases for tall table centre arrangements.

6

7

8

9

Bouquets with Wire Support

This wire support may not look very big, but it can hold many stems and allows you to create an oversized bouquet without the weight of the equivalent size of hand-tied bouquet.

Wire-supported bouquets can be chosen for a range of designs. The chicken wire provides a framework that helps to stabilise and give space to the stems within the design as you build.

Another benefit of creating bouquets this way is that you can put the bouquet down while making it if you need to. It can also be placed into a bucket of water at any stage and you can resume when ready. By contrast a hand-tied design needs to be taped first.

Tools

- Floristry scissors
- Wire cutters
- Gloves if required

Equipment & Sundries

- Chicken wire
- Flowers
- Foliage
- Twine

1. Cut a 20x20cm square of chicken wire to size. This is a good starting point and can be scaled up or down depending on your preference.

2. Roll your square into a cylinder.

3. Secure the cylinder by pushing the edges together with a few centimetres overlapping. Join together by twisting the edge wires onto the cylinder.

4. To close your cylinder, first push the ends in until they are flat, with the wires overlapping enough for joining them together. Then twist any open wires together for strength.

5. Your finished armature should feel secure and it should measure approximately 15cm long by 7cm wide.

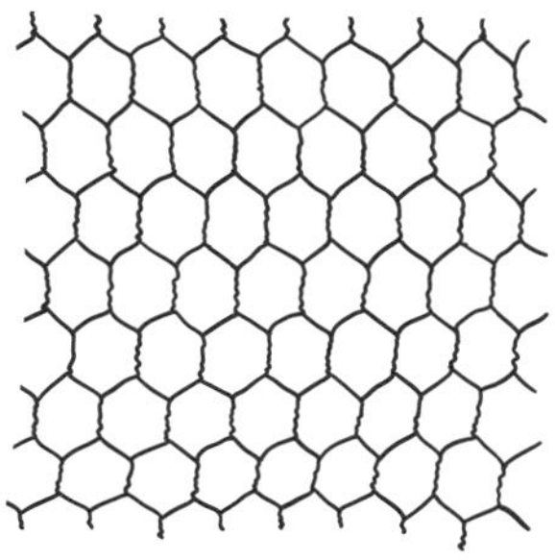

1

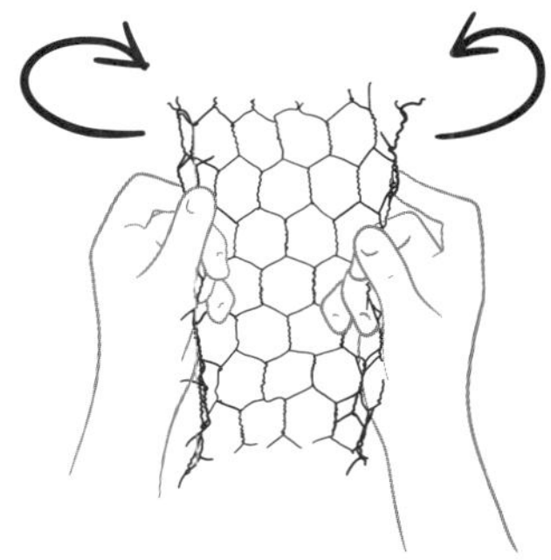

2

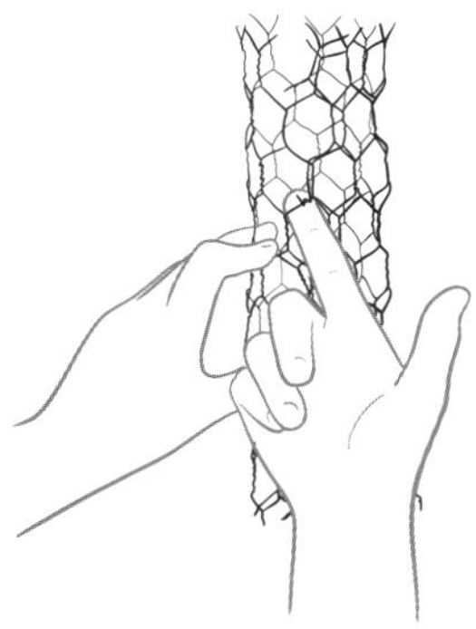

3

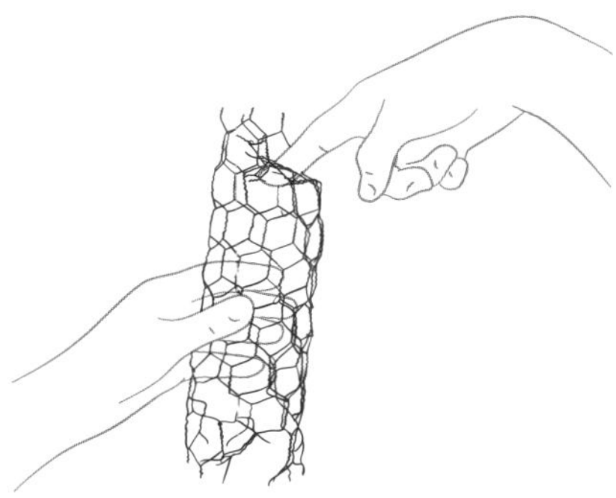

4

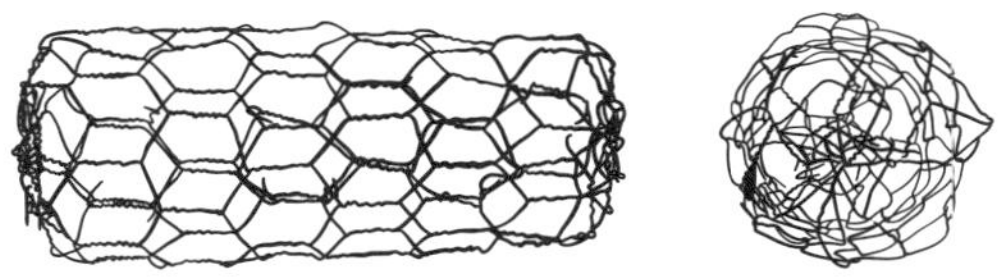

5

Bouquets with Wire Support (continued)

It is easy to focus more on the height and width of this type of bouquet, overlooking the depth. If you make sure to add elements that come forward (away from the bride, and back towards the bride), that will keep the design from becoming flat.

6. Lay out your conditioned flowers and foliage to make the process of designing into your armature as straightforward as possible.
7. Add foliage one stem at a time. Ensure that each stem goes through two apertures and feeds into your hand. This will create a clear tying point.
8. Working this way may feel a little unstable at first. As more elements are added, the structure will feel more secure. Larger elements can be twisted into position once you have built up the network of stems.
9. Next, add floral elements just the same way: through two apertures and into your hand.
10. Tie off with twine and cut stems to one length. About 15cm from the tying point is usually ideal but this is a matter of personal preference.
11. If needed, additional elements can be added to the outside of the framework which hide the mechanics. Adding shorter stems will not change the shape of your bouquet. Tie this off again to incorporate these stems, then place your bouquet into a vase or bucket.

Once it is made, keep the bouquet in a vase or bucket of water, preferably somewhere cool and dark. Ribboning is typically done on site.

Bouquets can be delivered in vases that can be reused or recycled.

6

7

8

9

10

11

Urns / Pedestal Arrangements

Urn arrangements can be created in the round or flat-backed depending on where they are being designed for, and they are often placed atop a pedestal or plinth.

It is good practice to create a liner for your urn arrangement. This ensures that any vessel will be watertight. Using a liner makes transporting your design easier as heavy vessels can be transported separately from the design. Once in situ your arrangement can be added to the vessel and the design can be tweaked if necessary. Trailing elements can be added, and the whole can be topped up with water. Once these chicken-wire-filled liners have been made, they can be reused as long as they're washed well after each use.

Tools

- Wire cutters
- Leather gardening gloves if desired

Equipment & Sundries

- Watertight or lined vessel of your choice
- Chicken wire
- Reel Wire or tape
- Gravel
- Bucket/Liner
- Fabric/Bubble wrap
- Plinth

1. Find a bucket cr insert that fits into your vessel securely. Ideally this will be at least 15cm high in order to support larger stems. If you are going to use a bucket as a liner, mark the place where the liner reaches the top of the vessel and cut the bucket to size.

2. Measure the width on the inside of the top of your vessel liner.

3. Cut chicken wire to create a square. Typically this is twice the width of the widest part of your liner.

4. Wearing gloves if they are needed, create a chicken wire ball, tucking the ends in underneath.

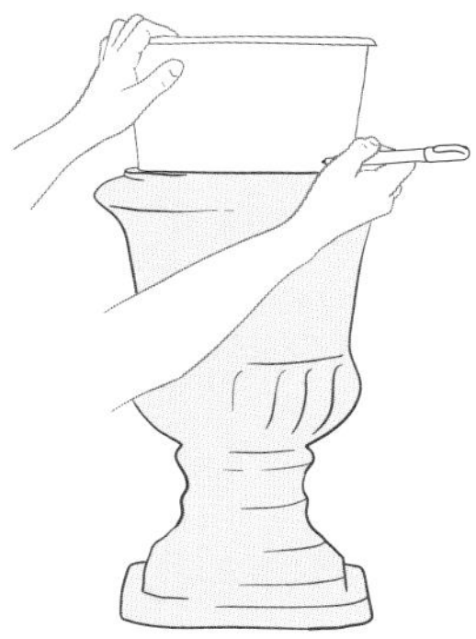

1

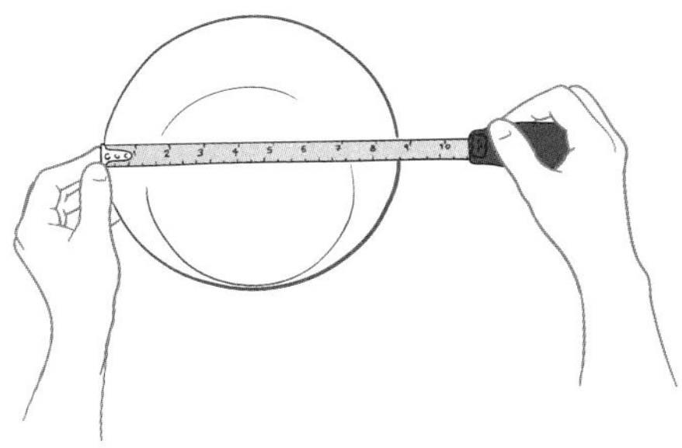

2

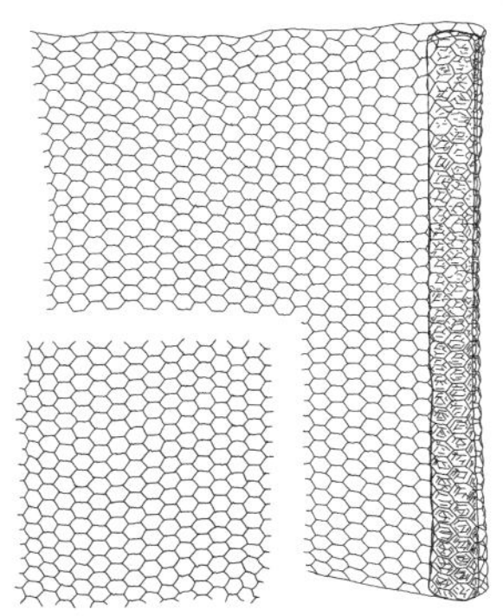

3

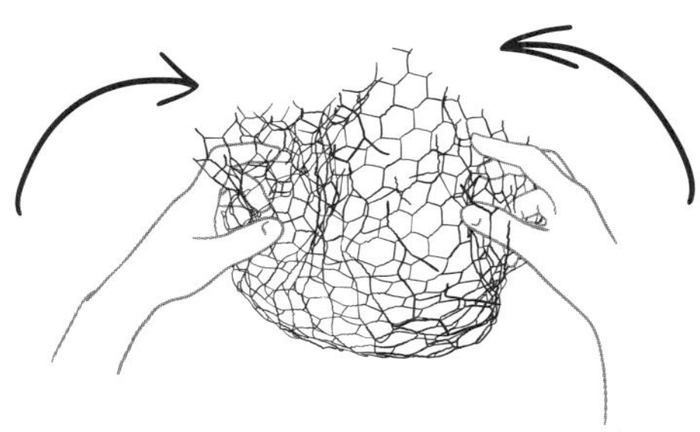

4

Urns / Pedestal Arrangements (continued)

5. Add stones or gravel to your vessel if extra stability is required. That may be necessary in windy conditions if the design is being used outdoors. Add your chicken wire ball to the vessel liner, making sure that it fits well. It should be a little proud of the top of the liner.

6. Secure your chicken wire ball into the liner using either reel wire or pot tape.

    - To use reel wire, carefully take a heated piece of uncoated reel wire or an uncoated stub wire and melt a small hole into your plastic liner at 4 equidistant points around the vessel and no less than a centimetre from the top.
    - If using pot tape, make a cross with the tape and ensure that it goes to at least 4cm over the edges of your liner.

7. If you are using wire, thread it through the holes that you have just made to form a cross. If using tape, pinch the sticky sides of the cross-shaped tape that is covering the chicken wire to itself so that it doesn't stick to the chicken wire or stems.

8. Place the prepared liner into your vessel. Fill with water and arrange your well-conditioned foliage and flowers into your vessel.

When adding foliage and florals place your vessel onto a plinth rather than a turntable. Initially stems may feel a little unstable but once you have a number of stems in place you will find that they create a network and lend support to one another. Once you have added all of the elements to your design it will feel secure.

Putting a piece of fabric or bubble wrap (which can be reused) in between your vessel and the liner will make removing the contents from the vessel easier after an event.

If you are arranging a design to fit a metal stand, there is no need to place your vessel into an urn but you may wish to use trailing foliage to cover the vessel.

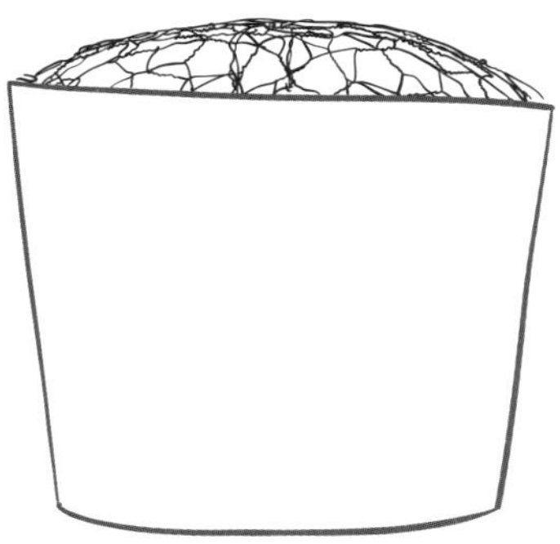

5

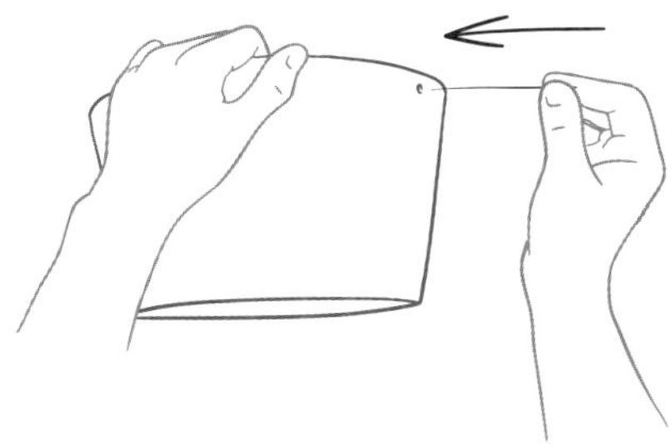

6

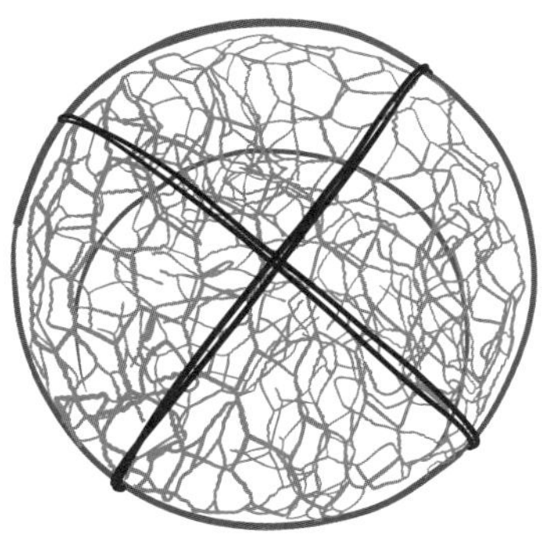

7

8

Meadow Boxes

Meadow Boxes can be used as the basis for a number of floral designs which are outlined on pages 58 and 59.

Tools

- Wire cutters
- Leather gardening gloves (if desired)

Equipment & Sundries

- Chicken wire
- Watertight or lined window planter/ trough
- Reel wire or twine
- Stones/Gravel

1. Measure your chicken wire. To work out the size of your chicken wire first measure the width of your vessel. The width of the chicken wire piece should match the width of your vessel so that it can be placed straight in. The length of the chicken wire piece required is around 60cm no matter the width of your vessel. Should you use a particularly deep vessel this will need to be scaled up. Cut to size.

2. Add 3-4cm of gravel/stones to your meadow box to ensure that it's stable and to lend support to larger elements of your design.

3. Completing steps 4 and 5 will result in a cylinder which has a layer in the centre to give support to the stems of your flowers and foliage.

4. Roll the cut chicken wire and place into the vessel to check that it fits securely. The roll can be tightened or loosened at this point if needed.

5. Secure the edge that is open onto the rolled chicken wire by twisting the free edges onto the remaining length of wire.

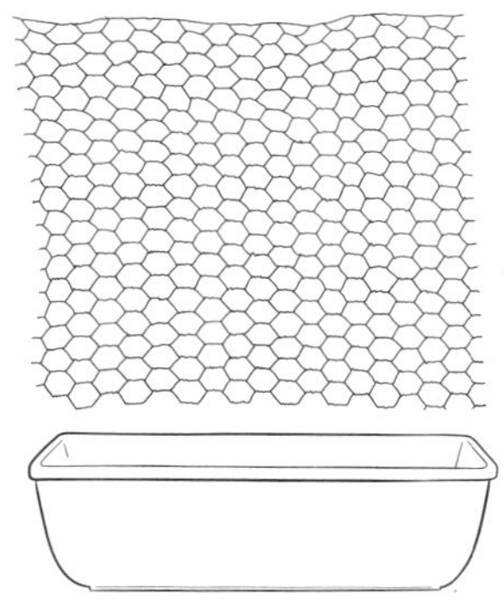

1

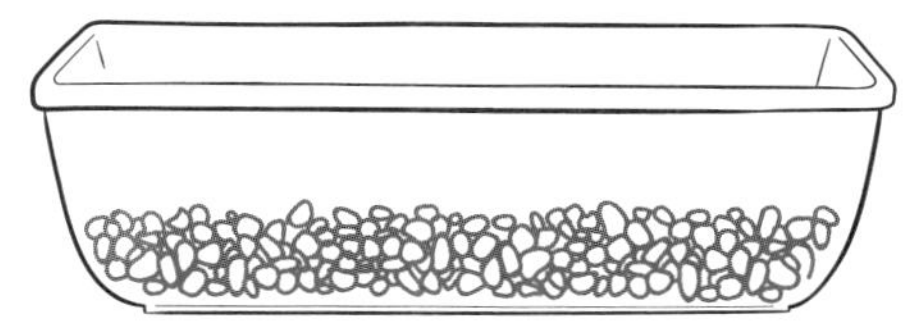

2

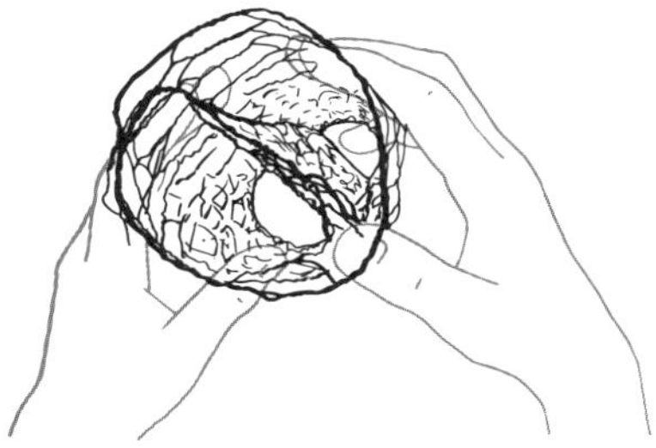

3

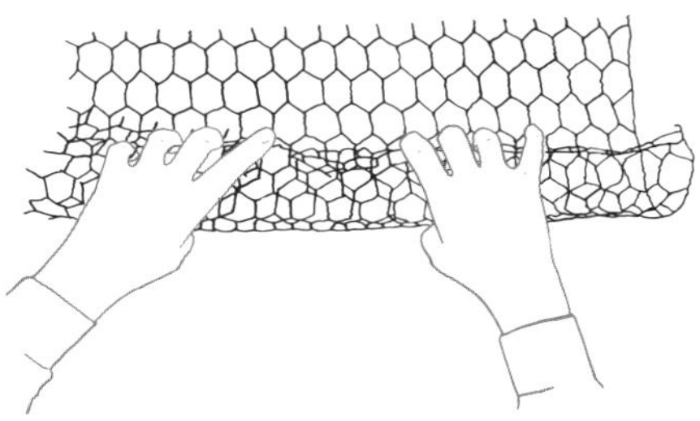

4

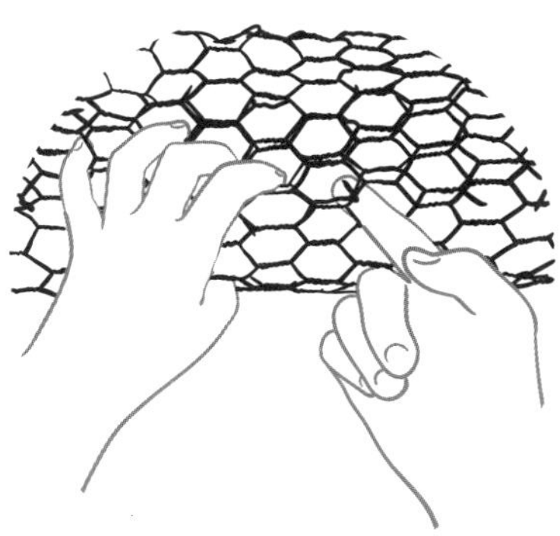

5

Meadow Boxes (continued)

6. Push the prepared chicken wire into the vessel, with the secured ends towards the base. Ensure that the layer in the centre of the cylinder illustrated in figure 3 remains horizontal. The top of the wire cylinder should be just a little proud of the vessel.

7. Tie twine on to your chicken wire and then around the entire vessel as shown to ensure the chicken wire remains in place. Reel wire can also be used in the same manner as shown for securing wire into liners in Urns on page 50 if appropriate for the vessel you have chosen. A third option is to use pot tape, though this is less long lasting than either the twine or wire options.

8. Your prepared vessel should look like the illustration in figure 8. Once ready to use, fill with water.

Arrange your flowers and foliage into your prepared vessel ensuring that the chicken wire and most of the vessel is covered.

The vessel should not be easily visible once you have finished designing into it. Your foliage and flowers should draw the eye, and the vessel should be there simply to hold them. Depending on personal taste, and depending where your Meadow Box will be viewed from, the planter can be hidden by wrapping it with a neutral fabric, with moss, or with hardy foliage.

For transporting these designs, empty some of the water out before loading onto a van or into a car. If you are installing on location, take any larger or trailing elements separately and add these once the design is in situ. Remember to top it up with water.

If your completed designs are to be placed onto a fragile or slippery surface, a non-slip mat can be placed underneath.

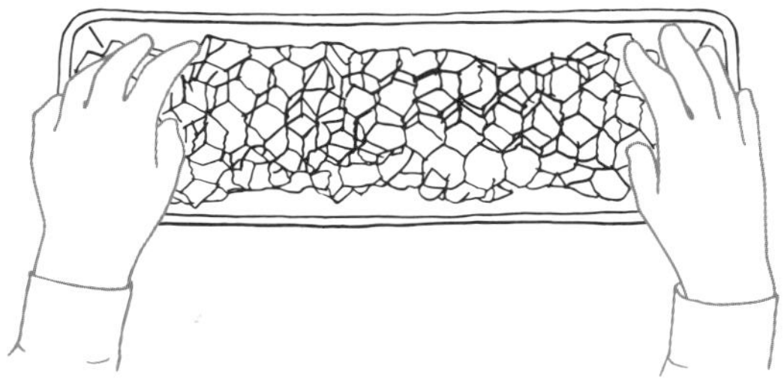

6

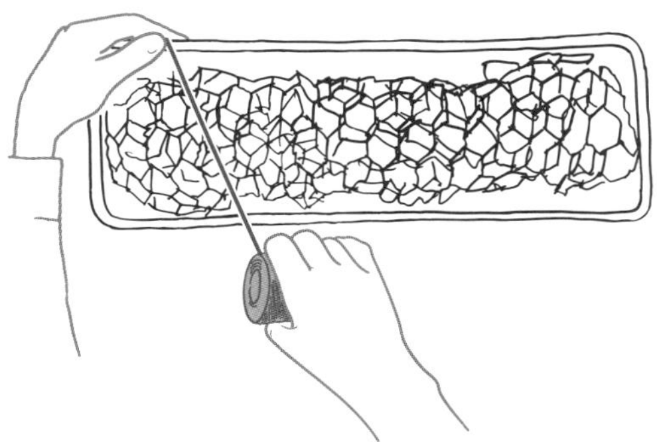

7

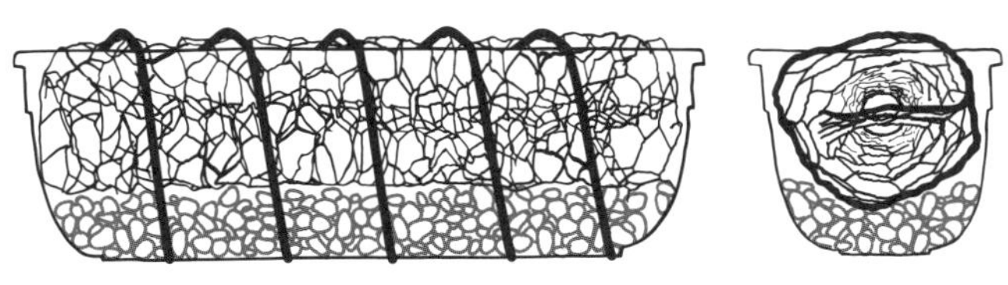

8

Uses for Meadow Boxes

Stairway designs

Your choice of vessel size will depend on the size of the stairway to be dressed. These can be placed on every step for an abundant design or staggered for a simpler design. Larger branches can be secured to bannisters if you have permission from the venue.
Hook-and-loop strapping or twine can be used for this to ensure that bannisters are not damaged in the process.

Mantelpiece arrangements

The weighting of your design should be carefully considered. Arrangements with large elements such as branches should be well anchored in the base of your vessel. You can ensure the design is secure by pushing branches through the wire and then additionally into the gravel/stones. Placing branches towards the back of your design, leaning against the wall behind, can lend extra support.
Larger vessels which have more weight to them can more easily support larger branches. Extra boxes can be used to extend your design as outlined.

Window/Alcove displays

These are made in the same way as both meadow boxes and mantel arrangements.
The chicken wire needs to be covered wherever it is to be placed. Your vessel may need to be covered all the way around rather than just at the front and sides as the back of your arrangement might be on display if it's in a window.

Aisle flowers

Meadow Boxes make good aisle runner florals and can be used even in warmer weather as the stems are able to drink. These are best suited to outdoor ceremonies, or ceremonies where there is a wide aisle. If required, meadow boxes can be re-purposed after a ceremony but carefully, because they are full of water.
As they are designed to be viewed from above when placed along an aisle, it's good practice to place your finished design on the floor once you have finished making it in order to check that your mechanics are hidden.

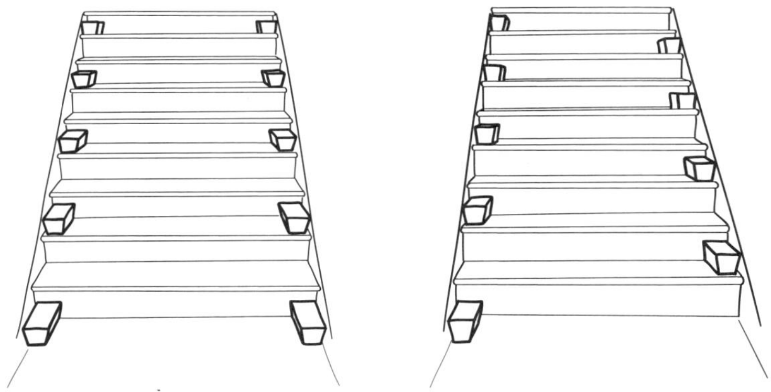

Stairways

Mantelpiece

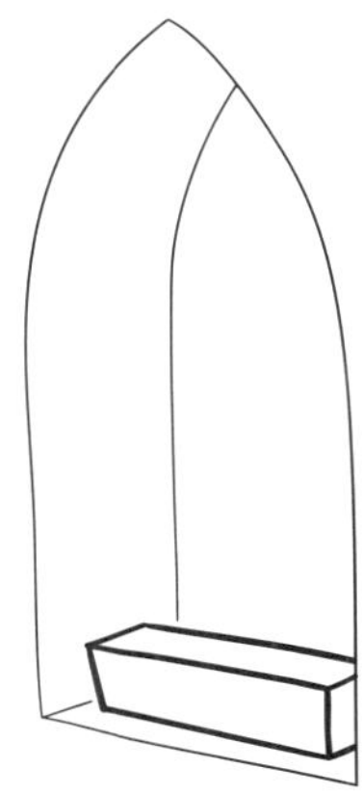

Window/Alcove

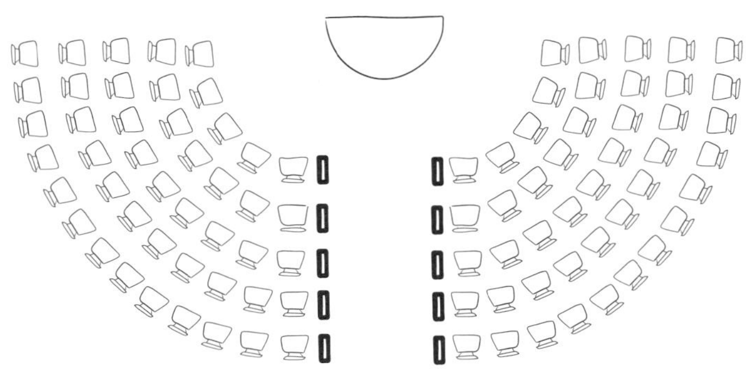

Aisle

Natural Wreath Bases

Many types of foliage are suitable for wreath bases, pliable leafless (or less leafy) foliage types such as ivy, willow or myrica gale are ideal for natural wreath bases.

It is advisable to work on an oil cloth or a table that can be wiped down easily as moss can be messy to work with.

Tools

- Floristry scissors
- Wire cutters
- Gloves if required

Equipment & Sundries

- Moss
- Pliable foliage
- Twine

1. Tie the end of a reel of twine to a piece of your chosen pliable foliage, leaving a tail of at least 5cm of twine to tie it off with when finished.
2. Add further pieces of foliage in the same direction, one at a time, adding the next stem a little further around your base each time. Pull the twine taut while spiralling it to hold the stems together as you progress.
3. Bend the joined section regularly as you build it up until you have created a circle the size of the base that you need. Continue adding stems to build the wreath base up until it is as thick as you need. Tie any loose pieces of foliage in. Tie off with the tail you left in step 1.

For designs that call for an unmossed frame (such as a dried wreath), stop at this point. For all designs that require moss, continue to follow these steps.

4. Tie the twine to the base. Now, working on one section at a time, take damp moss and cover the base generously, securing with twine as you go. Ensure that you have a good, thick layer of moss underneath, above, inside and outside your base. Once you have covered the base evenly, tie off the twine.
5. If you find that there are straggly pieces of moss, as is sometimes the case with grass moss, your wreath base can be trimmed. Spray with water and keep cool ahead of use.

Natural wreath bases are suitable for fresh wreaths. These are outlined on pages 64–65. Wreaths can be used for many events, including funeral work at natural burial grounds. Reel wire can be used in place of twine if preferred. For wreaths suitable for natural burial grounds, use twine rather than reel wire.

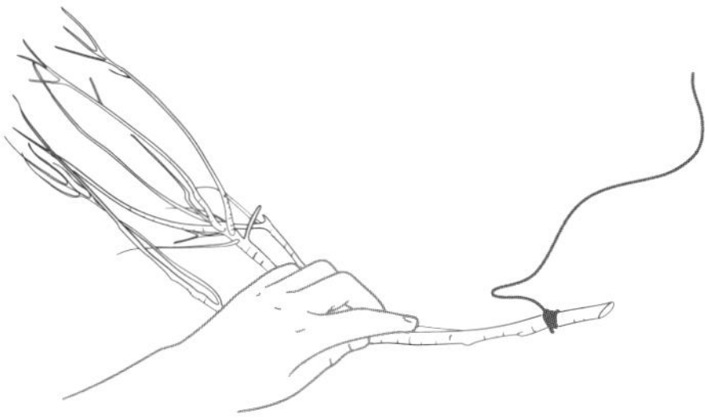

1

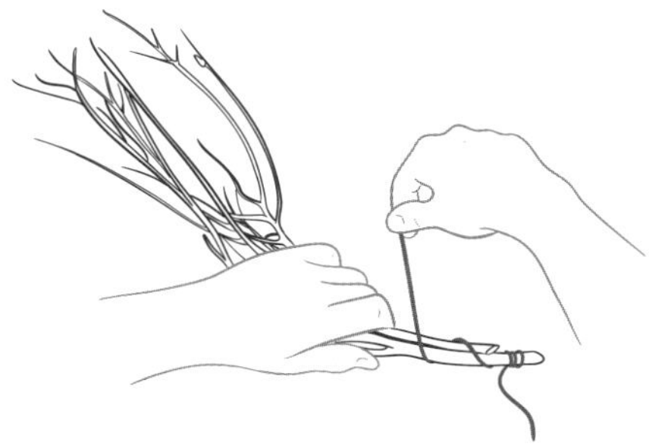

2

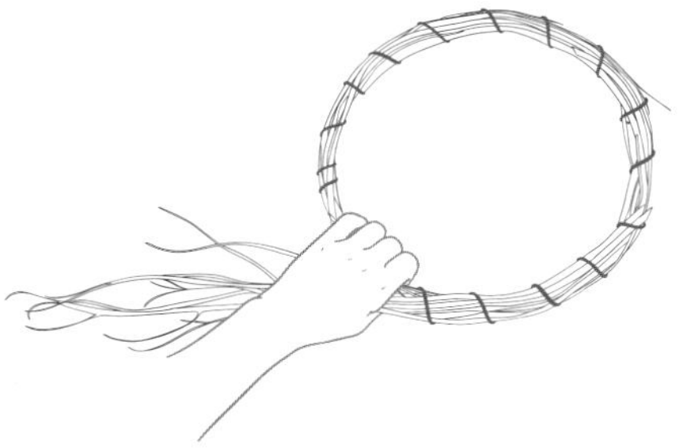

3

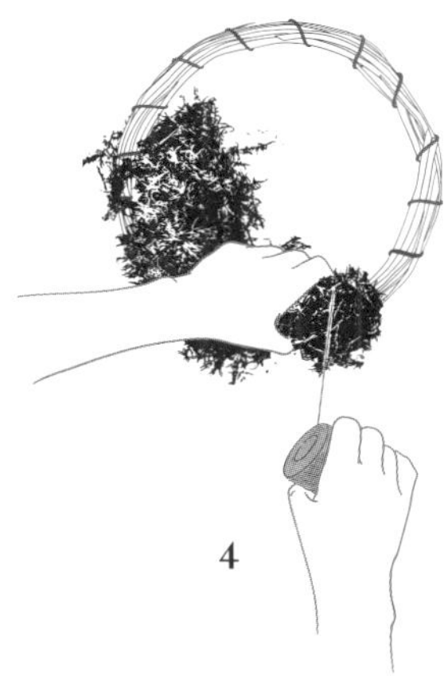

4

5

Wire Frame Wreath Bases

It is advisable to work on an oil cloth or a table that can be wiped down easily as working with moss can be messy.

Tools

- Floristry scissors
- Wire cutters
- Gloves if required

Equipment & Sundries

- Wire wreath ring
- Moss
- Twine or reel wire

1. Take one end of the twine or reel wire and attach it securely to the wire ring.

2. Add generous handfuls of damp moss to the wire wreath frame securing with reel wire or twine, making sure to pull the wire or twine over the top of the moss and underneath the base until the ring is covered fully, front and back. The moss should feel dense and secure. Pull the twine or reel wire as tightly as you can. It needs to be as secure as you can make it.

3. Once the ring is densely covered with moss, take the reel wire or twine around the same section two or three times. Secure the wire/twine to the ring as you did in step 1. Once completed, the moss should be thick and evenly distributed. You can add more moss and twine if necessary at this point. The moss should stay firmly on the ring when you pick the wreath up.

This type of wreath base is faster to make than a natural wreath base, as the ready-made rings are readily available from sundry suppliers. They are a cost-effective option and they can be reused, but please be aware that they are not suitable for natural burial grounds.

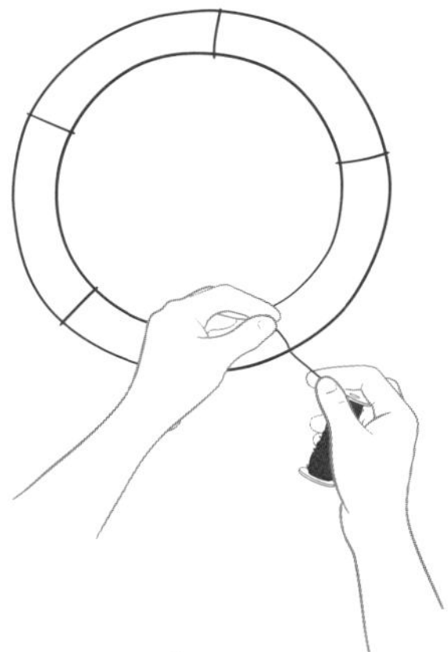

1

2

3

Fresh Wreaths

To create a fresh wreath, first create a wreath base. See the instructions for creating natural or wire framed wreath bases on pages 60 and 62.

Wreaths are incredibly versatile and can be created throughout the year to bring joy, to celebrate the seasons, and as tributes to loved ones. Fresh wreaths can be hung from doors. They can be placed flat to adorn tables. If you are using your wreath like that, place it on a plate. This will prevent marking or damaging any furniture or linen. Arrangements of this kind can feature a central pillar candle or an assortment of seasonal elements like fruits or nuts in the centre.

In large wreaths, flowers can be added in test tubes. Kokedama can be added to large scale wreaths if wired or tied into place. It is advisable to do this in situ. See page 26 for how to create kokedama.

Working with moss can be messy. It is advisable to work on an oil cloth or a table that can be wiped down easily.

Tools

- Floristry scissors
- Wire cutters
- Gloves if required

Equipment & Sundries

- Wreath base
- Flowers
- Foliage
- Twine or reel wire

1. Tie a reel of twine or wire onto your prepared wreath base. Spray the moss with water to ensure that it is fully hydrated.
2. Cut your well-conditioned stems into 10-20cm pieces with a sharp point, to help the stems go more easily into the dense moss. The length of your stems will depend on the design that you have in mind; shorter stems en masse will make for a denser, more even wreath; while longer, mixed-foliage elements will create a looser, more natural feel.
3. Add three pieces of foliage: one angled to the left; one in the centre; the third angled to the right to fully cover the base. Depending on your choice of foliage, full coverage may require more than three stems. Stems should be inserted into the moss by at least 3cm to ensure stability. If you are using any softer-stemmed foliage, a guide hole made with a knitting needle, skewer or spike can help the stems into the moss.
4. Keeping your twine or reel wire taut, wrap around the wreath base, securing your stems in place. Next, add another layer of foliage pieces as in step 3, overlapping the stems of the first layer. Then secure this layer as you did the first.
5. Continue in the same direction all the way around your wreath base (i.e. all clockwise or all anticlockwise) until you have completed the full wreath.
6. Hardy flowers and flowering, fruiting or berried foliage can be incorporated to your design for colour, texture and interest. Hardy flowers such as roses can be added to fresh wreaths in the same way as soft-stemmed foliage (step 3).

Fresh wreaths are typically only decorated on one side. Should you be displaying yours in a way that means both sides are visible, they can be greened up or fully decorated both sides.
To keep your wreath fresh for as long as possible it is advisable to hang it out of direct sunlight, and spray regularly with water.

1

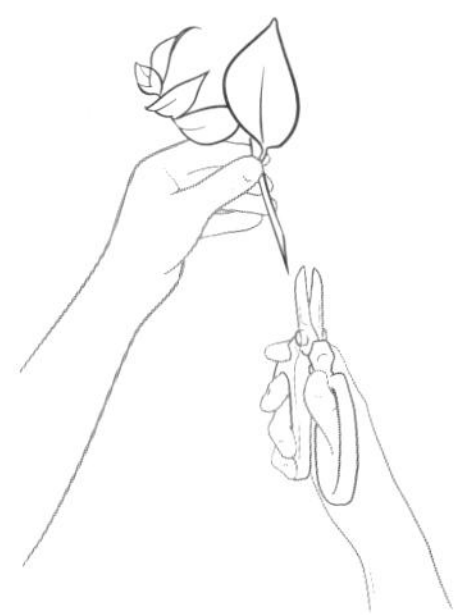

2

3

4

5

6

Wreaths with Advent Candles

For an Advent wreath, secure standard-sized dinner candles (25–30cm in length) to a wreath of 30cm to 40cm.

Pillar candles can be added in the same way as dinner candles but they will require more pins for stability.

It is advisable to work on an oil cloth or a table that can be wiped down easily as working with moss can be messy.

Tools

- Floristry scissors
- Wire cutters

Equipment & Sundries

- Heavy-gauge wire
- 4 x candles
- Pot tape
- Fresh wreath

1. Place your fresh wreath onto your workbench. (Guidance for making this can be found on pages 64 and 65.)
2. Take four 20cm long heavy-gauge wires (18–20 gauge is ideal). Bend each wire into a U-shape (or hairpin), either by hand or using long-nose pliers. You will need four of these hairpin-shaped wires for each dinner candle.
3. Hold one of the hairpin-shaped wires against the candle as shown.
4. Tape to the candle with pot tape, then add three more wires evenly around the base of the candle in the same manner.
5. Push each candle into the fresh wreath in turn so that they are evenly spaced around the wreath. They should feel secure in the densely packed moss. If you find that the wires come out of the bottom of your wreath bend these protruding wires back into the wreath base with the pliers.

Add any further decorations. Place your wreath on a plate or tray to protect furniture or linen.

Traditionally four candles are used in an advent wreath, three of one colour and one of a different colour.

These wreaths are created as a decorative item and as such if these are for a client, it should be outlined to a client that lighting the candles is entirely at the client's own risk. If the wreath is for you, consider placement carefully and ensure that you never leave a burning candle unattended.

1

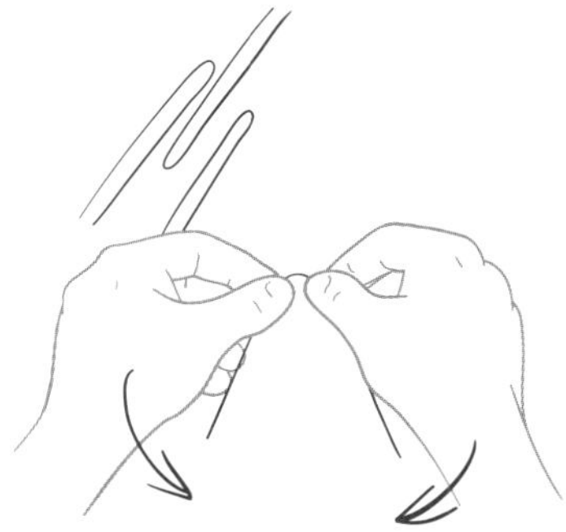

2

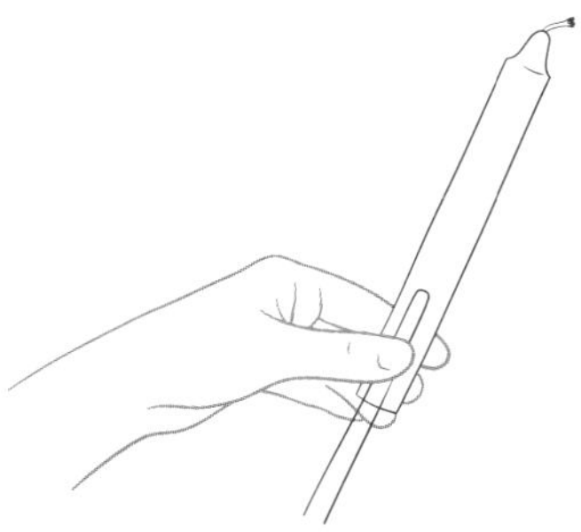

3

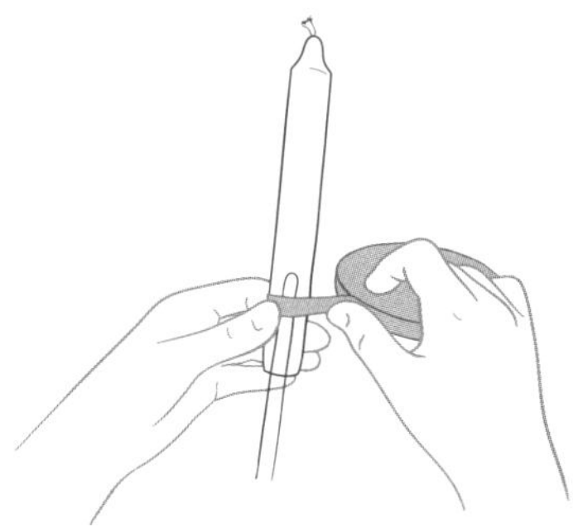

4

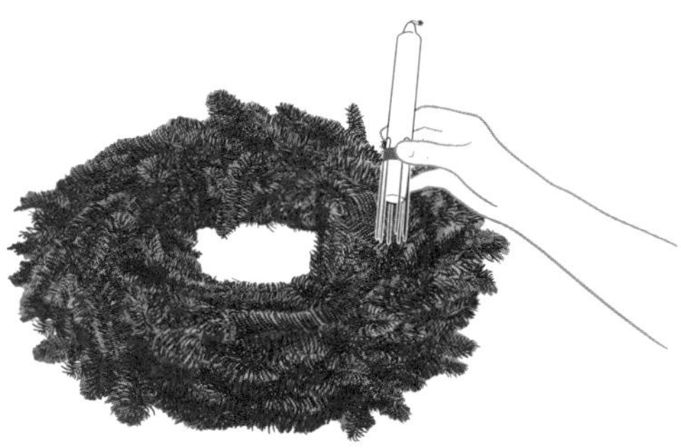

5

Dried Wreaths

If using a metal hoop as a base, it is advisable to tape the section that you want to decorate using waxed florist tape to give you more purchase and to stop the bunches from sliding down the hoop. Taping a small section where you plan to add your ribbon also helps to keep it from sliding out of place.

If the wreath is to be held rather than hung, the entire base should be decorated and not just the front. This will take a good deal more dried material. You'll probably need six or seven of your groups of flowers rather than the three groups mentioned in step 5.

Tools

- Floristry scissors
- Fabric scissors

Equipment & Sundries

- Willow wreath base, metal hoop or embroidery hoop
- Reel wire or twine
- Dried flowers, seed heads, grasses
- Ribbon

1. Place your wreath base or hoop onto your workbench. Details of how to create a natural base can be found on pages 60–61. Do not moss your base.

2. Lay out your ingredients, then cut stems down to lengths of between 10cm and 20cm depending on your design. Longer elements can be incorporated so long as the stems are strong enough.

3. Gather small bunches of dried elements in your hand, (carefully) pulling stems up and down to create pleasing combinations

4. Secure the bunches with twine or reel wire and trim their ends for a neat finish.

5. If you are new to creating dried wreaths, it can be useful to lay your bunches out to see which combinations work best next to one another. Attach the reel wire or twine to your base. Using your wire or twine, securely fasten your first bunch on to the base by taking the wire or twine over the tie point of the bunch and going around a few times, wrapping the twine or reel wire tightly to secure them.

6. When adding each new bunch, ensure that you are covering the stems of the previous layer, making certain that you add all the bunches in one direction (i.e. all clockwise or all anticlockwise). To create a full wreath which covers the front of the base, add your first bunch slightly at an angle to the left, add the next bunch straight and add the following bunch slightly to the right. Continue in this manner until you get back to where you started, or as far as you'd like to go. (Half wreaths or wreaths with just a small section decorated can look great.)

7. To suspend your dried wreath, add ribbon or twine by folding a piece in half. Loop it around the base, then thread it back through itself. Finish by knotting the loose ends or tying a bow.

8. Hang up the wreath and once it is in situ, extra elements can be tucked in securely if needed.

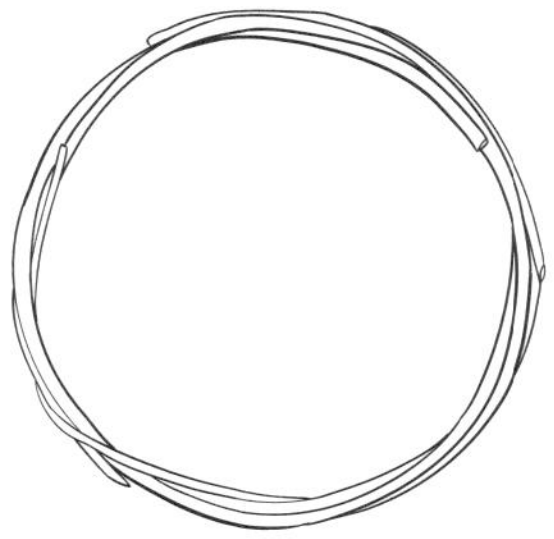

1

2

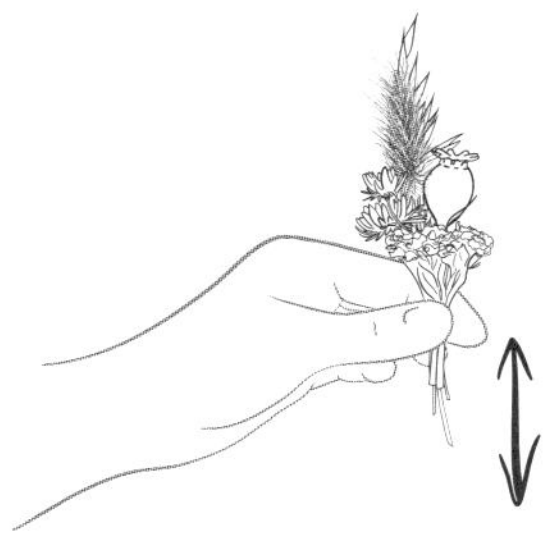

3

4

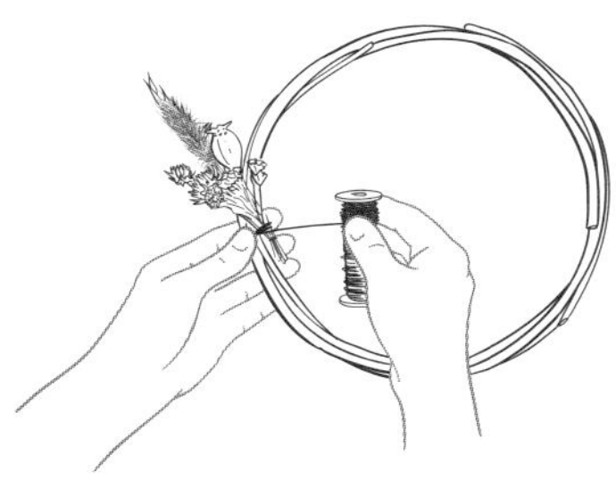

5

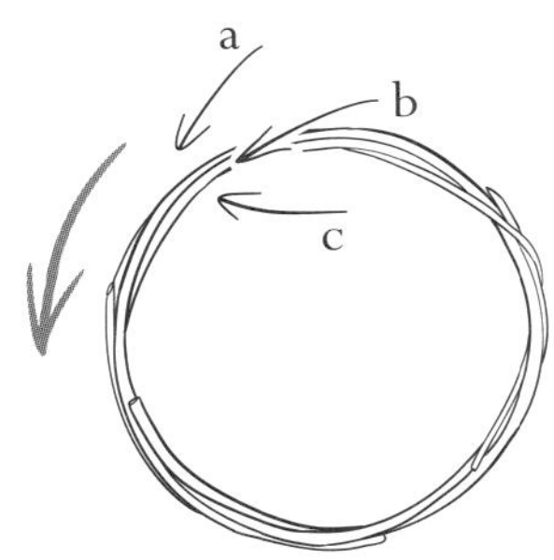

6

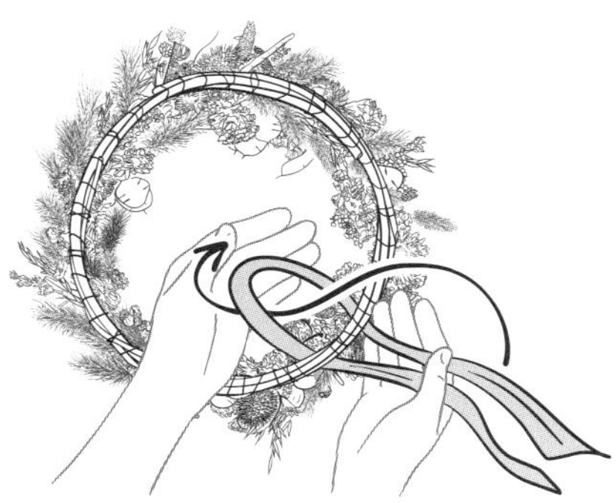

7

8

Garlands

Garlands can be made to any length. Should you need longer garlands, it's useful to create them in 2m lengths for ease of creating stem counts, so that they are easy to handle, and for transport.

For long garlands, follow the steps, but tie off each section rather than finishing the final sections (steps 5, 6, and 7). When in situ, wire the sections together and to finish the garland, turn its final section to face the opposite direction, creating a tapering end. Wire the ends together.

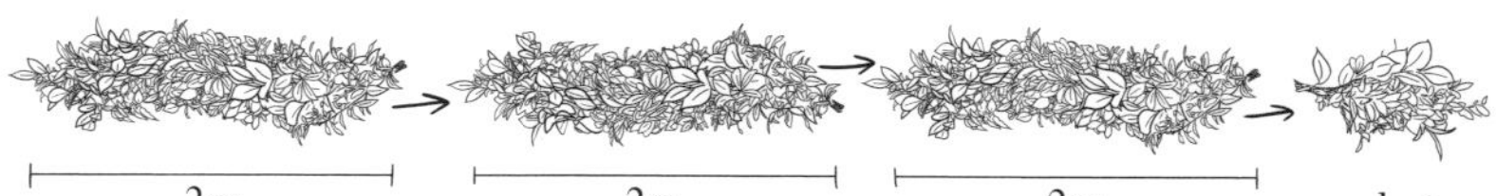

The key to making good garlands is your choice of materials. Designs can be simple, using one type of foliage, or more abundant garlands can be created by incorporating foliage with a mixture of textures. The length of the stems you choose is important. Short stems will create neat, dense garlands. Longer stems can be used to create looser, larger garlands that can become the base of a floral installation. Branches can be strapped together with hook-and-loop strapping or wired together for the base of installations.

The following guide is based on standard sizes of foliage from the UK market. You may need to adjust the ratios depending on the sizes of bunches and ingredients you do use. Make a small test garland to ascertain how much of each ingredient is appropriate for your style and needs.

For simple table runners: 1 bunch of foliage per 90cm of garland.

For standard garlanding: 1 bunch of foliage per 60cm of garland.

For full, abundant foliage garlanding: 1 bunch of foliage per 30cm of garland.

Tools

- Floristry scissors/ Secateurs
- Wire cutters

Equipment & Sundries

- Reel wire or twine
- Foliage
- Hook-and-loop strapping (Velcro)

1. Allocate your well-conditioned foliage.
2. Choose a piece of foliage that tapers nicely. Then, taking a roll of reel wire or twine, secure the open end of the wire or twine onto the branch by wrapping it around the stem a few times and twisting the wire onto itself or knotting the twine securely. Whether using twine or reel wire it is a good idea to tie off sections regularly to ensure that if one piece of wire or twine were to break your whole length of garland would not be compromised.
3. Cross the stems of the foliage over one another ensuring that you leave stems long enough to add the next pieces of foliage to them. To create an even garland, add stems from three directions (left, middle and right) and bind tightly with reel wire or twine.
4. Moving down a little, add the next layer of foliage pieces. These should overlap the stems of the first pieces. As you continue to add foliage your stems will form a backbone. Keep adding foliage pieces until you have the length required. Then tie off securely.

1

2

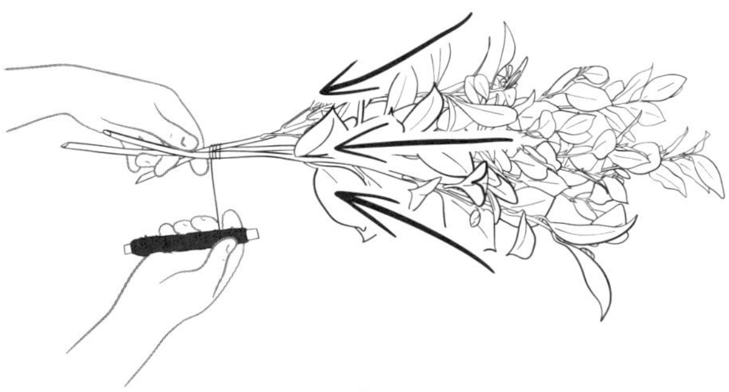

3

4

Garlands (continued)

5. Next, make a small section of garland. This is a shorter version of the garland you have already made. Lay it out so that your garland sections are 'stem-to-stem'. It can be useful to trim any long stem ends so that you have less stem to hide.

6. Bring the garland pieces together, overlapping them so that the stems of both ends are hidden as much as possible. Wire or tie the stems of the backbones of the garland to the rest of the foliage until it is fully incorporated to the garland and feels secure.

7. To create seamless garlanding, take a few more stems of foliage and attach each one individually, wiring on to the existing stems and creating an even finish without any discernible join.

Garlands can be used as the basis for table runners, swags, arches and hanging installations.

Use foliage that you know will last well out of water. Adding a variety of types of foliage will make for a more natural feel.

Hook-and-loop strapping can be used to attach garlands to bannisters, hoops, or other fixing points.

Garlands can be made ahead of use so long as they are kept well hydrated. Spray them well with water and use bin bags or plastic sheeting to keep them fresh. These bagged garlands can be carefully stacked somewhere cool, ready for transport.

5

6

7

Floral Garlands

Foliage garlands are the basis for floral garlands. Foliage garlanding can be bought pre-made from wholesalers or made: as per page 70.
Floral garlands can be used along tables, attached to bannisters, for installations such as hoops and to dress structures such as Arches, Chuppahs and Mandaps.

Consider the conditions where your floral garlanding is to be installed, and how long your flowers will need to last, when choosing which flowers to use. Consider whether they need to be water-tubed or taped.

Tools

- Floristry scissors/ Secateurs
- Wire cutters if using wire

Equipment & Sundries

- Foliage garland
- Reel wire or twine
- Hook-and -loop strapping (Velcro)
- Waxed tape
- Water tubes
- Flowers

1. Separate your flowers into the number of stems needed for your design per 50cm of garland to ensure that your flower count is consistent throughout the garland.
2. Put your foliage garland into position. To secure it, hook-and-loop strapping works well in place of reel wire, cable-ties/zip ties, and it will not cause damage to wooden bannisters, or delicate materials. It is a good alternative where wire would be inappropriate within the building or venue. Hook-and-loop strapping is strong, reusable and easy to remove after an event.
3. Flowers that need hydrating should be added to water filled test tubes. For hardier flowers such as roses or tulips which hold well short term without the need for hydration, waxed tape can be used to seal the stems rather than using water tubes.
4. After tubing or taping your stems, tuck your flowers into position in the garland. Attach the tubes or stems to the foliage using reel wire and ensure they are secure by twisting the ends of the wire together.
5. Check the design to see whether any of the tubes are visible. If they are, you can wire or tape small pieces of foliage onto your tubes within the garland to camouflage them.

For large installations, it's useful to have buckets ready stocked with water filled, capped tubes.

1

2

3

4

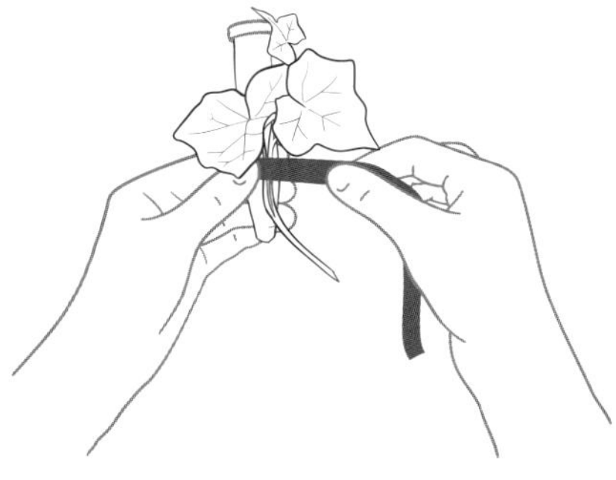

5

Arches with Flowers and Foliage

Tools

- Floristry scissors
- Secateurs

Equipment & Sundries

- Arch structure/ Weighted uprights
- Weights
- Reel wire or twine
- Hook-and-loop strapping
- Test tubes
- Grave spikes
- Foliage
- Flowers

1. Assemble your freestanding framework ensuring that it is adequately weighted. Cast-iron Christmas tree stands are ideal for weighting frames or poles as they are heavy and relatively small and usually have the capacity to hold some water. Alternative methods for weighting structures include sandbags, weights, and wooden poles fixed into buckets of ready-mixed, fast-setting concrete.

2. Use foliage which holds well out of water to cover the base of your structure. Ivy is ideal as it can be wrapped around the bases.

3. Attach branches of well-conditioned foliage to the structure using hook-and-loop strapping. This needs to be foliage that you are confident is going to hold up well out of water for the duration of the event. If you are using large branches that need a water source, grave spikes filled with water are ideal. Either these can be attached to the structure, or you can attach them to pieces of foliage that you have added already. Smaller branches can be added to water-filled stem tubes to ensure hydration.

4. Take some water filled stem tubes and add florals to them. Then attach the flower-filled tubes to the foliage which is already in place, use reel wire and twist securely. If you are using flowers that are hardy enough to be taped rather than tubed for the duration of your event, those can be attached to foliage garlanding in the same manner.

5. Check to see whether any of the test tubes or grave spikes are visible. If any are, wire or tape small pieces of hardy foliage onto the tubes in your design to hide them from view.

To create a 'broken arch' or a half arch, weighted upright posts can be dressed in the same way as the posts for a full arch.

It is advisable to secure a 'broken arch' or half arch to a fixing point if you can, and preferable to secure it at points higher up the design. If no fixing points are available, weighting is key, particularly when working outdoors.

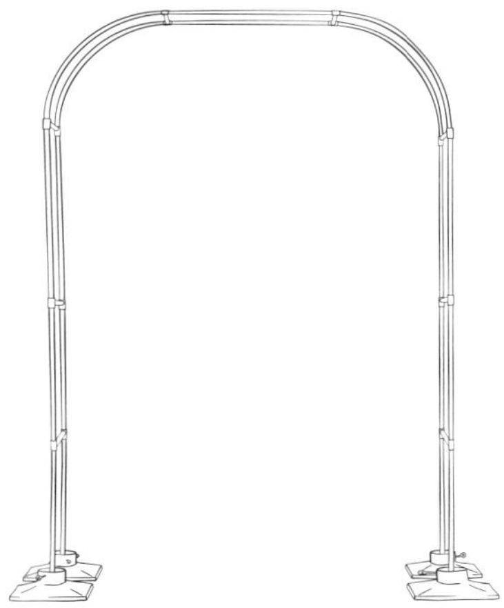

1

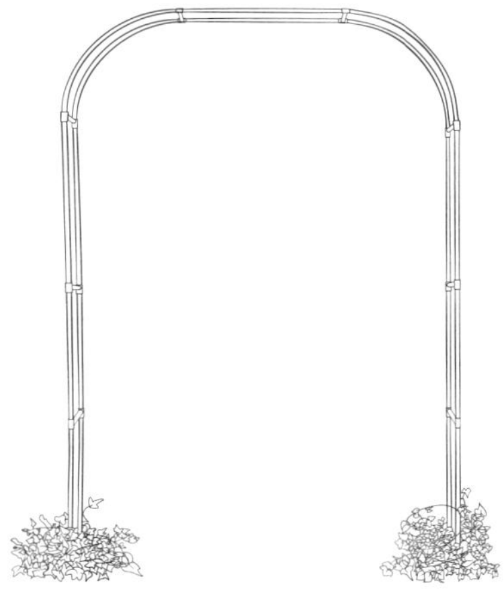

2

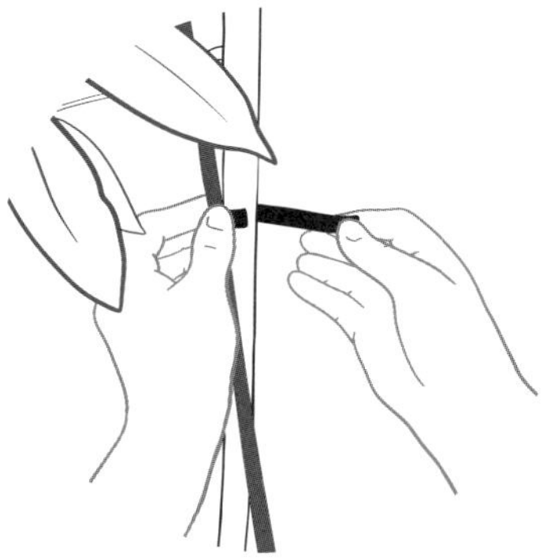

3

4

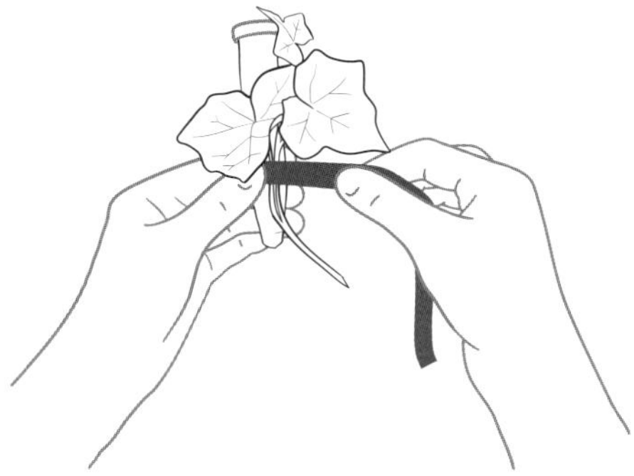

5

Flower-filled Arches

A mixture of roses and spray roses works particularly well for this design. Ahead of creating the mechanics for this design, assemble your free-standing framework ensuring that it is adequately weighted. Cast iron Christmas tree stands are ideal for weighting frames or poles as they are heavy and relatively small. Alternative methods for weighting structures include sandbags, weights, and wooden poles fixed into buckets of ready mixed, fast-setting concrete.

Tools

- Floristry scissors
- Secateurs
- Wire cutters
- Fabric scissors

Equipment & Sundries

- Arch structure/ Weighted uprights
- Weights
- Chicken wire
- Reel wire
- Waxed florist's tape
- Hook-and-loop strapping
- Test tubes
- Focal flowers
- Dried hydrangea (optional)

1. Unroll the chicken wire to the length(s) that you require according to your design. Cut to size. Next, cut the chicken wire width. This should be at least 60cm. For full arches, creating three separate sections will make the process easier than making one long section.

2. Fill the chicken wire with foliage. This can be leftovers from conditioning, responsibly foraged, pruned, or inexpensive greenery. The foliage will support the stems of the flowers and will not be visible in the finished design.

3. Roll the chicken wire to create a foliage-filled cylinder no smaller than 20cm across.

4. Join the lengths of the chicken wire securely as shown, using the open ends of the wire.

5. Wrap the chicken wire mechanics around the sections of the structure that you want to flower.

6. Secure the mechanics to your framework at regular intervals with wire or hook-and-loop strapping.

7. Add florals to water-filled stem tubes, then push flower-filled stem tubes securely into the apertures of the chicken wire. Depending on the time that your design is needed for, roses can be used without tubes if they are taped at the ends to prevent water loss.

8. Check to see whether any of the test tubes are visible. If they are, add more tubed or taped flowers until you have built up the level of fullness that you are looking to achieve.

Dried hydrangea heads can be used as a base layer for this design. Their stems can be pushed through the chicken wire, into the foliage, and they will not require hydration. This can be useful for covering mechanics. Other hardy flowers or foliage can also be used to hide mechanics if desired, and leaving the leaves of roses on can soften any view of the mechanics underneath. This is not a budget design as it takes a large number of flowers to complete. It is suited to wedding ceremonies with statement pieces such as Arches, Mandaps or Chuppahs.

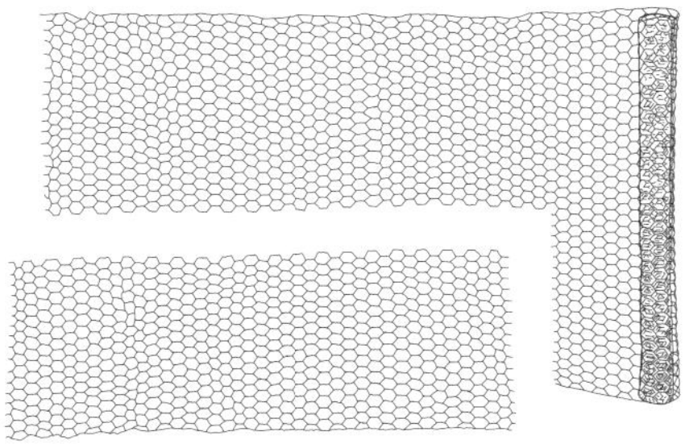

1

2

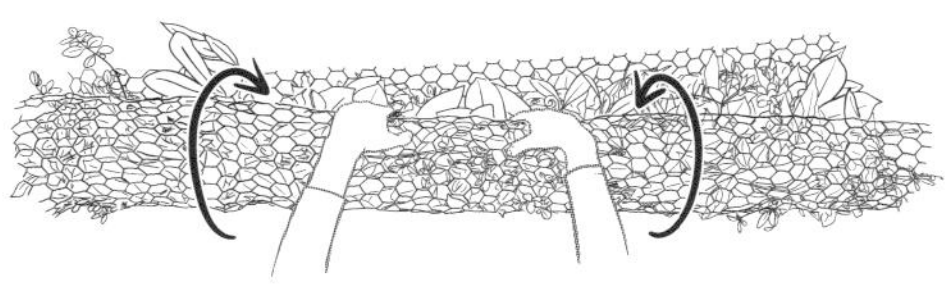

3

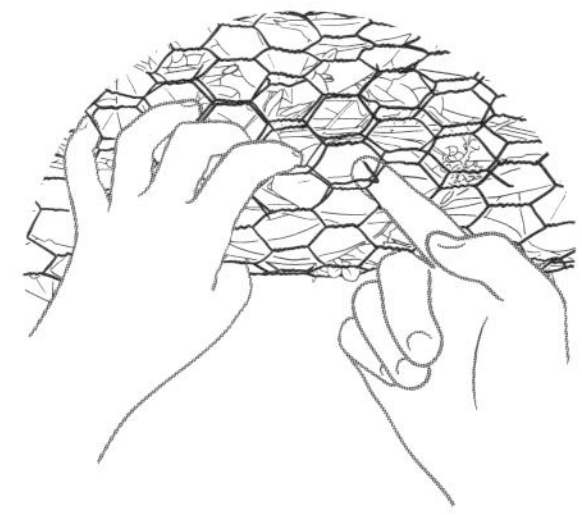

4

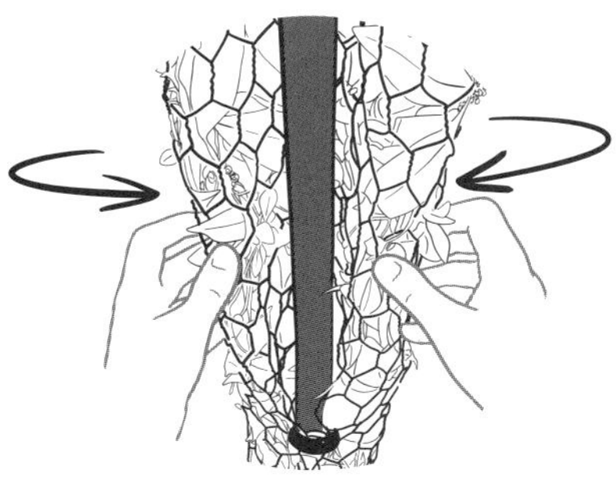

5

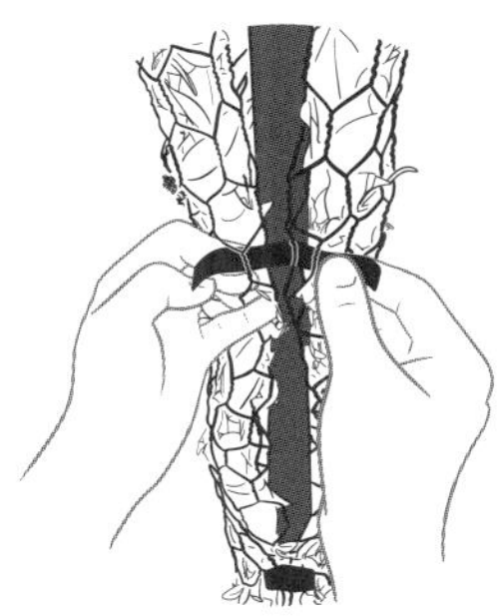

6

7

8

Suspended Hoops

As with all of the designs covered in this manual, the style of design is up to you. This method works whether you're looking to create a formal style or a loose unstructured hoop. Hoops can also be completely covered in hops, ivy, dried stems or any natural elements that will hold well out of water.

Check the maximum weight allowed from any fixing points at the venue and whether you will need to provide your own pulley system. If the venue or a marquee company are providing a pulley system for your installations, it is worth requesting a loop at the end of the rope so that you can attach your installation safely, quickly and easily.

Tools

- Floristry scissors
- Fabric scissors

Equipment & Sundries

- Hoop, ropes and fixings
- Use twine or reel wire, or hook-and-loop strapping (Velcro)
- Garlanding or large branches
- Foliage
- Flowers, tubed or taped

1. Attach the hoop to the point from which you will be suspending it using a shackle or a carabiner. Tie the ropes off to secure the hoop to approximately shoulder height so that you won't have to overstretch as you build your design. Having the hoop at this height also allows for a clear view of the hoop.

2. Attach branches of hardy foliage to the hoop, using hook-and-loop strapping. Ensure that you add stems in the same direction. This can be done with reel wire, but it is a quicker, easier process with hook-and-loop strapping. The branches can be attached both inside and outside the hoop as well as underneath and on top of the framework.

3. Adding larger elements first helps to build up the overall shape. Work with the shapes of the elements that you are using. Next add bushier elements that provide more coverage if required, though this will depend on your style.

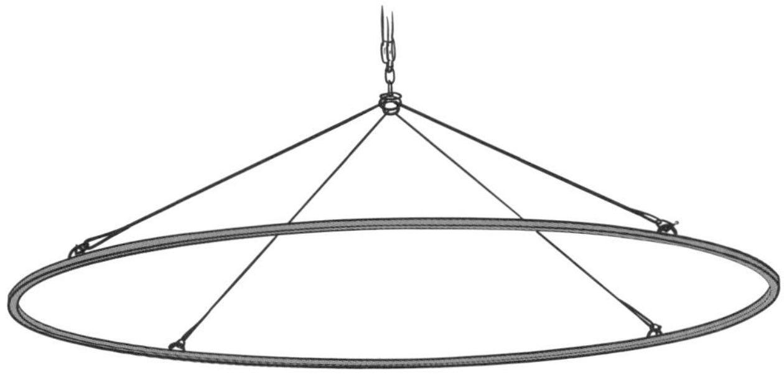

1

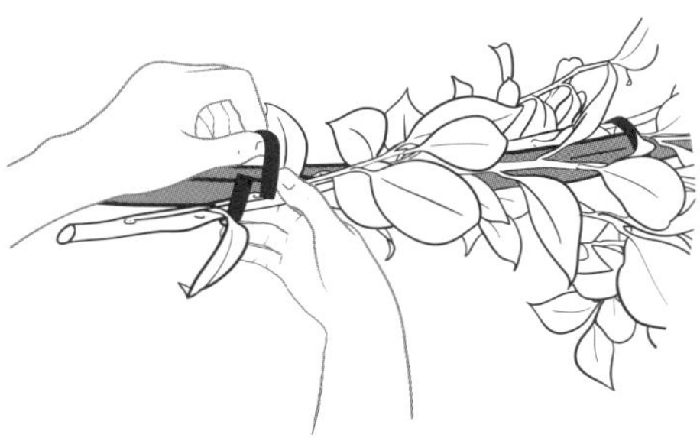

2

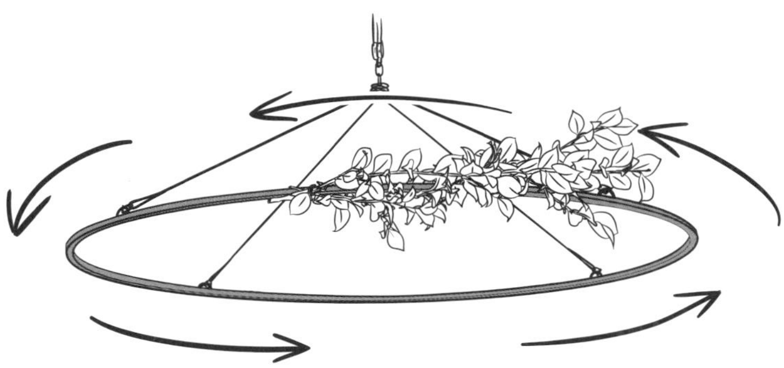

3

Suspended Hoops (continued)

4. Add flowers and any less hardy foliage stems to water-filled test tubes. Attach these filled tubes to the foliage branches that are already attached to the frame using reel wire or hook-and-loop strapping. Some flowers (such as well-conditioned roses or tulips) will hold well out of water for at least 12 hours; these flowers can be taped and added into your design without the need for test tubes.

5. Check to see whether any of the test tubes are visible. If any are, wire or tape small pieces of hardy foliage onto the tubes in your design to hide them from view.

6. Spray well with water, then pull your hoop into position, and tie off securely.

As with all of the designs covered in this manual, the style of design is up to you. This method works whether you're looking to create a formal style or a loose unstructured hoop.

4

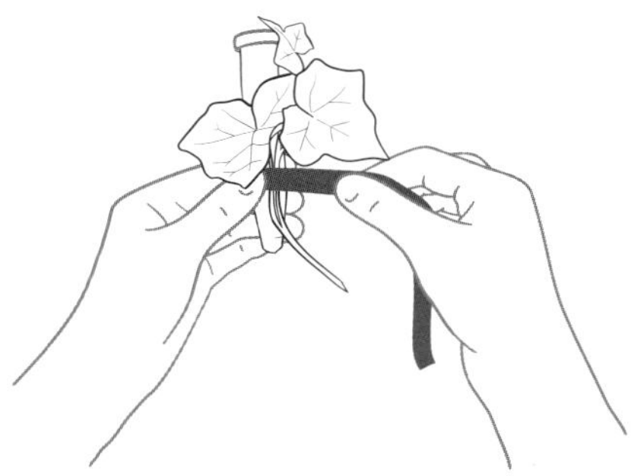

5

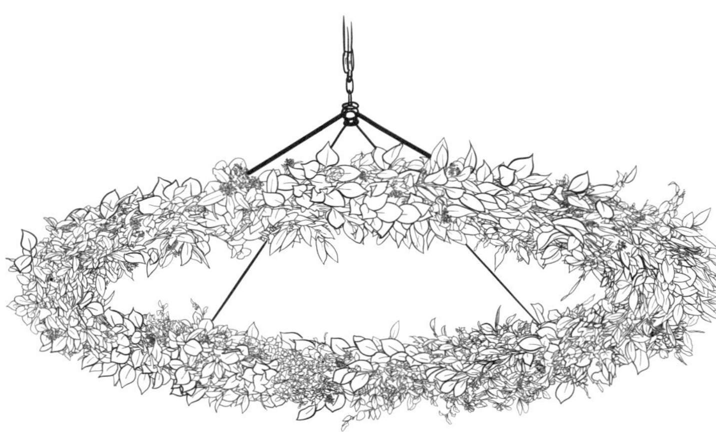

6

Floral Clouds

The mechanics outlined below are suited to a cloud with an overall width of between 1m and 2m, depending on your design this can be scaled up or down to suit your needs.

Tools

- Wire cutters
- Secateurs
- Floristry scissors
- Fabric scissors
- Leather gardening gloves (if desired)

Equipment & Sundries

- Wood
- Drill (optional)
- Carabiner
- Chicken wire
- Reel wire
- Hook-and-loop strapping (Velcro)
- Heavy-duty fishing line – ideally 35-55lbs weight
- Test tubes
- Foliage
- Flowers

1. To create the base mechanics of your cloud take a piece of wood 50cm long. Ideally it will be at least 5cm wide and a minimum 2cm deep. If you can, drill two holes in each end. If this is not possible, tie your fishing line around the wood. We recommend drilling holes and threading fishing line through these holes for security.

2. Thread heavy fishing line through the holes to create a swing with a loop at the top. The fishing line can be as long or as short as works for your design. A length of 1–2m is generally sufficient to create the illusion of a 'floating' cloud.

3. Measure your chicken wire and cut to size. For mechanics in the size outlined above, use a rectangle of 85cm x 50cm.

4. Place your wood in the centre of the chicken wire ensuring the fishing line is upward. Wrap the chicken wire rectangle around the wood to create a cylinder. Then join at the top, ensuring that the fishing line comes out of this join. (See figure 7 for how your mechanics will look once finished.)

5. Once the top is secure, close the ends of the cylinder, twisting any loose chicken wire ends together for strength.

6. Use hook-and-loop strapping to secure the chicken wire on to the wood, ensuring that it goes under the wood and over the chicken wire with a 10cm overlap of strapping for strength.

7. Hang your 'swing' up from a fixed point or a pulley system. Using a carabiner, attach the fishing line loop to your fixing point so that the wooden part of the 'swing' is at shoulder height.

1

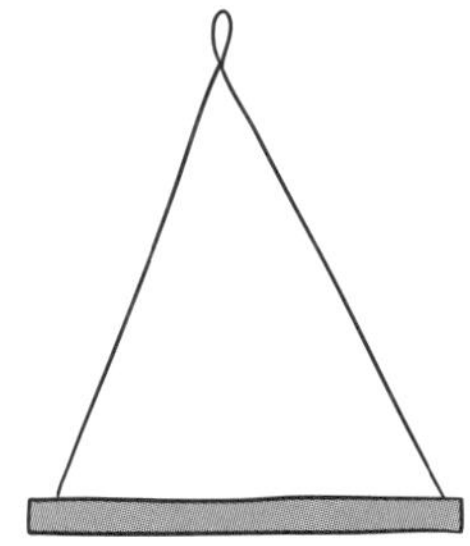

2

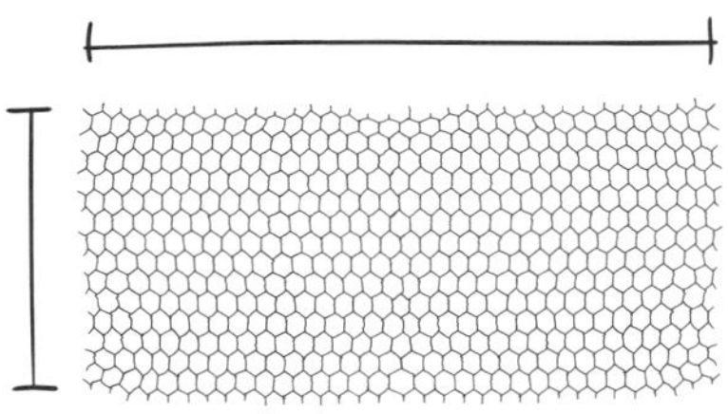

3

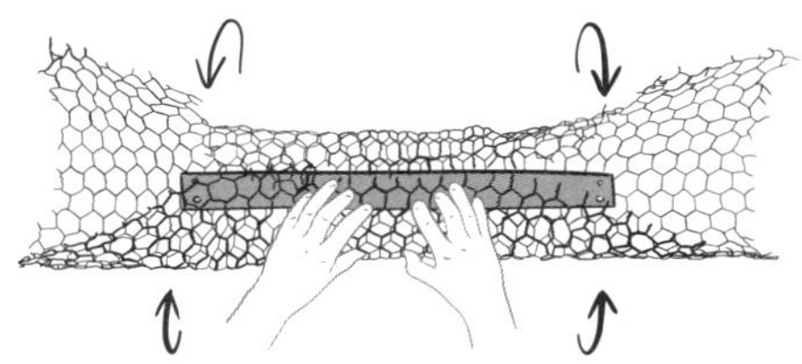

4

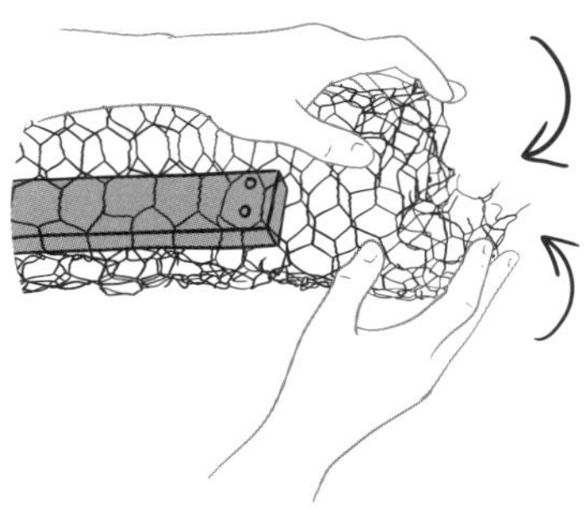

5

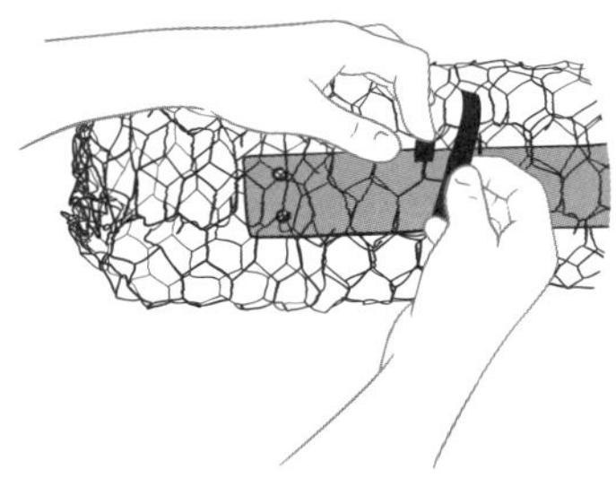

6

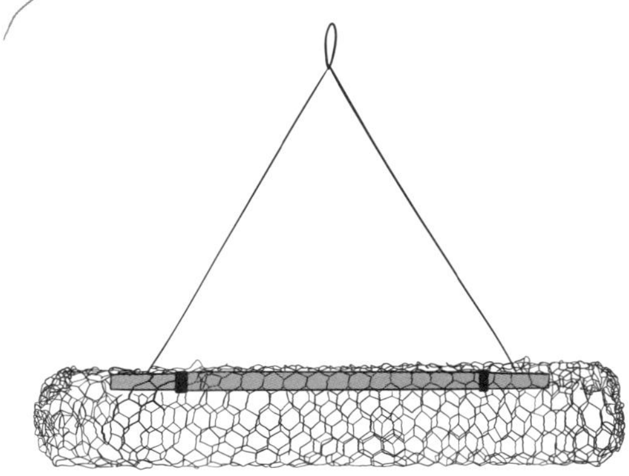

7

Floral Clouds (continued)

8. When adding foliage, start with your larger elements to create a base shape. Ensure that your stems pass through at least two apertures; the chicken wire can be bent and manipulated around branch ends for security at this point. If necessary, foliage stems can be further secured with reel wire once in position. There is no need to remove any leaves from your foliage lower down the stems, as these can help to give your stems more grip, and that helps to keep elements in place.

The more stems you add, the more secure the cloud will become.

9. Add foliage pieces around the whole of the chicken wire in this way until you have good coverage. Once you are happy with the shape of the cloud, check to see that everything feels secure. If the stems feel loose, add shorter stems to build up the network of stems inside the cloud without changing the shape that you have created.

10. Add your test-tubed flowers. The tubes should be pushed through an aperture, if the tube does not feel completely secure use a little reel wire or hook-and-loop strapping to secure the tube onto the stem of a piece of foliage which is already in place or on to the chicken wire itself. Taped, hardy elements such as tulips or roses can be inserted without the need for test tubes if appropriate for the temperature of the venue and the longevity required. Softer, less hardy foliage can be water-tubed and added at this stage.

11. Spray liberally with water and then pull your cloud up into position.

Check the maximum weight allowed from any fixing points at the venue these are to be installed at, and whether you will need to provide your own pulley system.

Ideally flower clouds are made in situ. If you have a short window of opportunity for installation, the clouds can be made ahead of time, sprayed with water, wrapped carefully with light plastic sheeting (or two large bin bags) to seal the moisture in, then suspended from inside a van. Florals are best added on site (sheeting/ bin bags can be reused if handled carefully).

On site, if there are two points available for you to suspend your structure from, you can attach the fishing line through the holes at each end, then attach it to your two fixing points. This will stop your cloud from spinning or twisting around.

Flower clouds can also be made using dried elements following the steps here. Bear in mind that they do hold an enormous number of stems.

Filling the inside of the chicken wire cylinder with foliage at step 4 will create a network of stems, which will give the finer stems of dried elements a little more purchase.

Ensure that there are no candles placed underneath and look into fireproofing if you are creating any installations using dried elements.

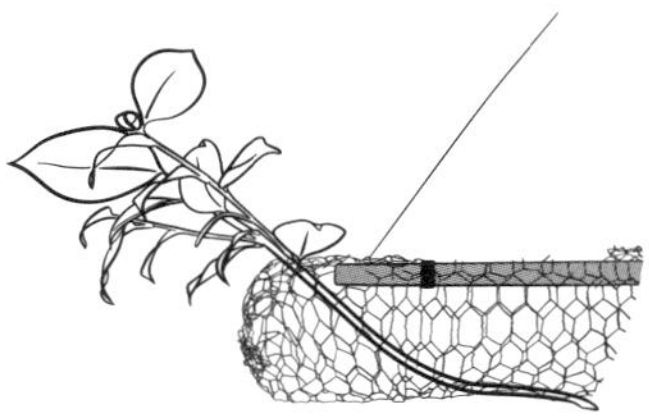

8

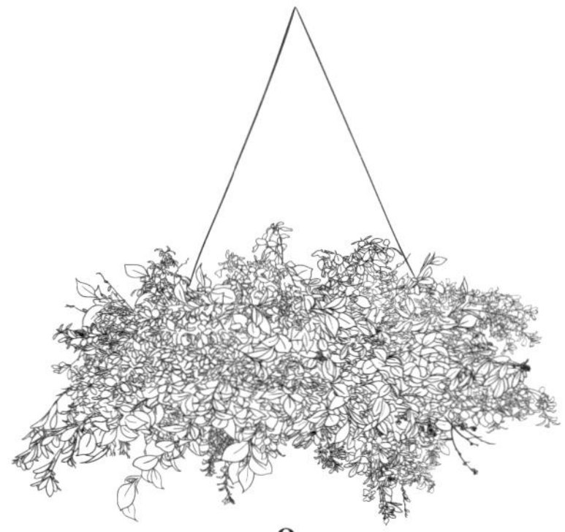

9

10

11

Sheafs

This is in effect a flat-backed bouquet. It can also be made with spiralled stems and, if preferred, flowers can be added alongside foliage rather than afterwards.
Funeral sheaves can be made 48 hours ahead of delivery if placed into a bucket of water and kept cool.

Tools

- Floristry scissors

Equipment & Sundries

- Flowers
- Foliage
- Twine

1. The profile of a traditional funeral sheaf is lower at the end and builds in height towards the tie point. Use longer pieces initially and build up the shape by using progressively shorter elements towards your tie point, creating the shape as shown.

2. Begin with your longest foliage pieces, tapered shaped pieces make for a pleasing start to the design. The initial piece should be the full length that you intend your design to be.

3. Continue adding further stems of foliage, to the left, middle and right, building layers up evenly. Each new layer of foliage should be brought down the design a little, while ensuring that all stems reach past your tie point.

4. Once you have a shape that you are happy with, begin adding your floral ingredients, tucking through the foliage and ensuring that they reach past your tie point.

5. When you have added all of your flowers and are happy with your design, trim the ends, tie off with twine and place in a bucket of water.

It is advisable to supply a piece of non-slip mat for funeral designs.
These can often be collected after use.

1

2

3

4

5

Crosses

For designs in moss, use hardy foliage. Hardy flowers such as roses or tulips can be added in advance; more delicate varieties should be added on the day of delivery. If you're unfamiliar with the longevity of flowers and foliage, experiment with materials ahead of designing to ensure that you have elements that are appropriate.

Working with moss can be messy, it is advisable to work on an oilcloth or a table that can be wiped down easily.

Tools

- Floristry scissors
- Knitting needle, plant spike or skewer

Equipment & Sundries

- Willow
- Flowers
- Foliage
- Twine
- Moss
- Oilcloth
- Non-slip mat

1. Cut your willow to size. A ratio of 3:4 works well for crosses. For example, if you are looking to create a 40cm long cross, the horizontal pieces that cross over would be 30cm.

2. Lay out a cross shape with half of your vertical pieces underneath the horizontals and half on top. The number of stems you need will depend on how thick they are and on how substantial you want your cross to be.

3. Tie the willow together with twine as shown to create a secure cross shape. For larger crosses, use more pieces of willow for extra strength.

4. Trim the willow if required then tie the ends together with twine.

5. Generously cover your willow with a thick layer of damp moss, securing it in place with twine as you go. Check that your cross is fully and evenly covered in moss. If there are any less generously covered sections, add a little more before moving on.

6. Add well-conditioned foliage to cover the base. Cut your stems at a sharp angle in order to insert stems easily into the moss. Most foliage stems will go in unaided if cut at a sharp angle. If your foliage is softer-stemmed, you can create a guide hole first with a knitting needle, plant spike, or skewer. For security, stems should be inserted into the moss by at least 3cm.

7. Lay out a cross shape with half of your vertical pieces underneath the horizontals and half on top. The number of stems you need will depend on how thick they are and on how substantial you want your cross to be.

These can be made 48 hours ahead of delivery if sprayed well and kept cool. It is advisable to supply a piece of non-slip mat for funeral work, these can often be collected for reuse.

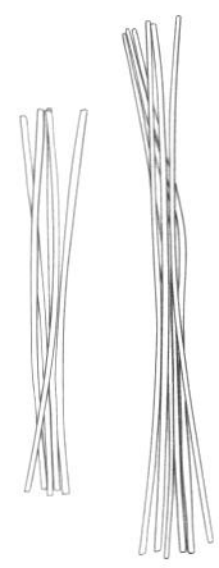

1

2

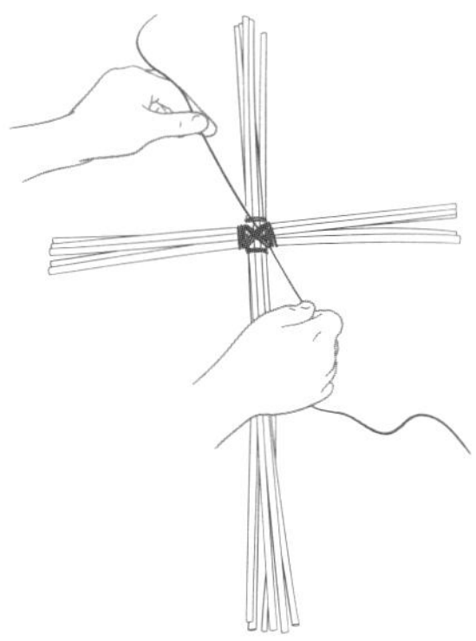

3

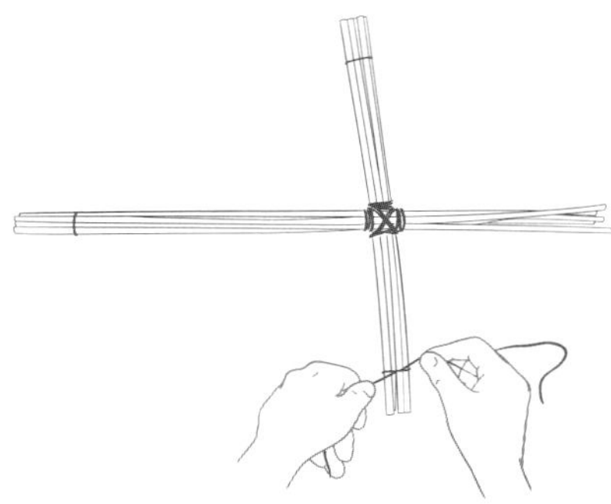

4

5

6

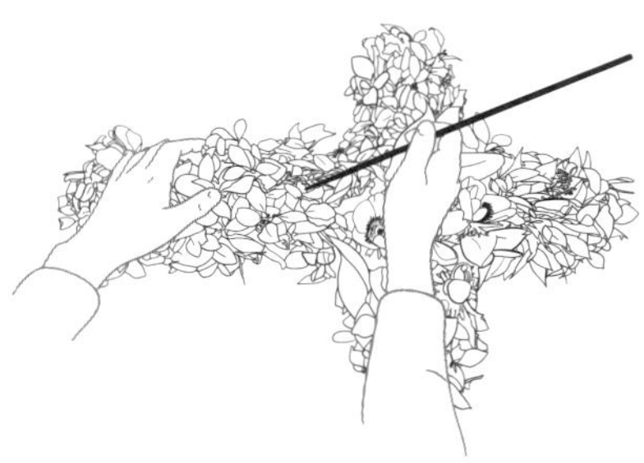

7

Coffin Topper

This funeral work has been designed to be completely biodegradable in order to be suitable for natural burial grounds. Be mindful of adding any elements which could include plastic or metal sundries or equipment so that you don't inadvertently compromise the biodegradability of your design.

The wooden plank used in this set of instructions is 74cm x 13cm and no less than 1.5cm thick. A plank this size fits three of the 9cm x 15cm rectangular trays when they are put on lengthways. Depending on the length of foliage used and the design, these mechanics are suited to a 3–4 foot (91cm–122cm) long topper. The design can easily be scaled up or down depending on the size of topper that you need to create and the size of palm leaf trays that you use.

These designs can also incorporate small plants and planted materials such as herbs and bulbs tucked in to the palm leaf trays.

Working with moss can be messy. It is advisable to work on an oilcloth or wipe clean surface.

Tools

- Floristry scissors
- A knitting needle, plant spike or skewer

Equipment & Sundries

- Plank
- Fabric
- Twine
- Moss
- Oil cloth
- Palm leaf tray
- Foliage
- Flowers
- Non-slip mat

1. Take your plank and wrap with fabric.
2. Using twine secure the fabric to the plank.
3. Take your palm leaf trays and generously fill with damp moss.
4. Secure the damp moss onto the trays with twine.
5. Next, tie the three trays onto your fabric covered plank securely using twine
6. Fill your mossed trays with water.
7. Add well-conditioned foliage to the moss filled trays to create the desired shape of your design ensuring that every stem is cut at a sharp angle. This will help stems to go into the moss easily. If your foliage is softer stemmed, you can create a guide hole first with a knitting needle, plant spike or skewer. Most foliage stems will go in easily unaided. All stems should be inserted into the moss by at least 3cm for stability.
8. Once you have added the desired amount of foliage to your base, add your well-conditioned floral elements. Soft-stemmed flowers will go into the moss more readily if you create a guide hole with your knitting needle, plant spike, or skewer. Once inserted these stems will feel secure so long as they have been inserted far enough into the moss.

These can be made 48 hours ahead of delivery if sprayed well and kept cool. It is advisable to supply a piece of non-slip mat for designs such as these. Non-slip mats can be often be collected in order to re-use.

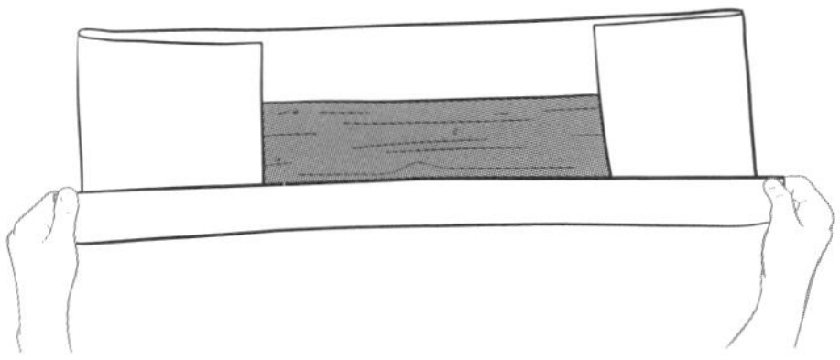
1

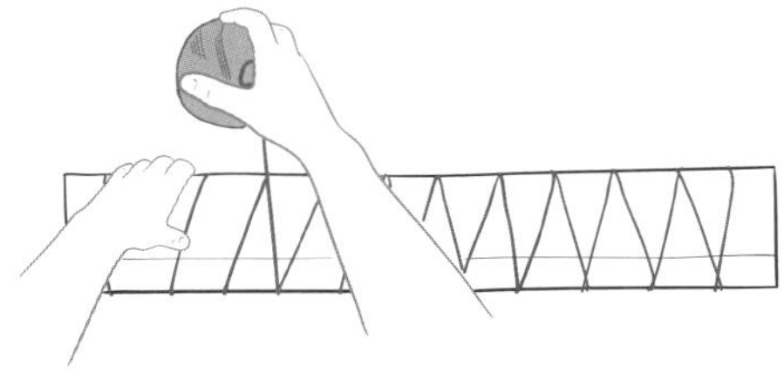
2

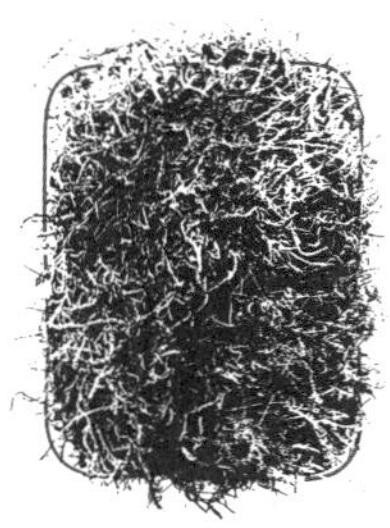
3

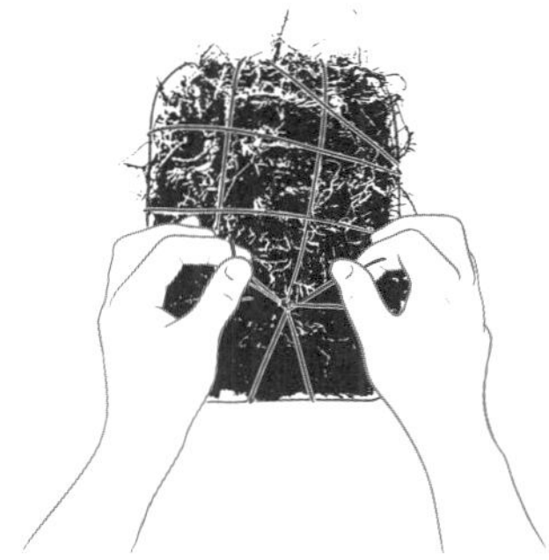
4

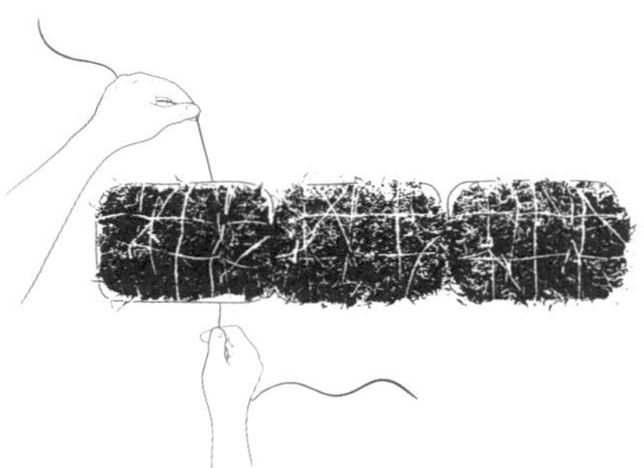
5

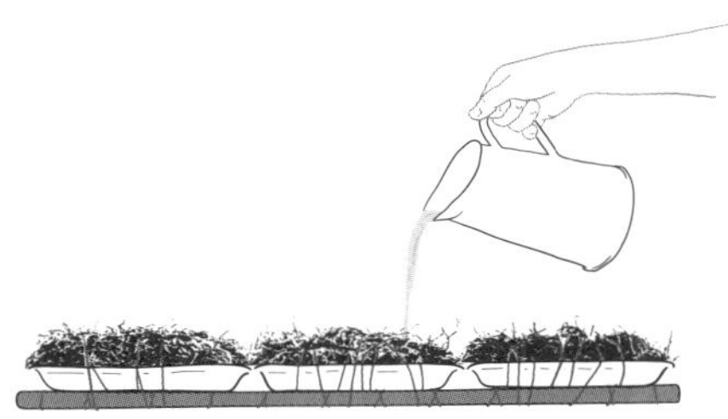
6

7

8

Working Off Site

Ahead of the install date, check that you have access to water, tables to work at, and whether there is storage space for items to be left for a tear-down after the event.

Check for local events and possible road closures around the time of the event, and the availability of parking.

Your wellbeing and that of any staff working for you must be considered too. Are there adequate toilet facilities? Is there access to drinking water? Is there somewhere that you or your staff can buy food and drinks?

A checklist of your kit, which can be checked before setting off to the venue and again before leaving to ensure nothing has been left behind, can be useful. If you are in business, make sure your insurance is up-to-date.

These are the things we wouldn't be without when installing florals off site

- A trolley with which to move your equipment
- First aid kit
- Venue and client/planner details including addresses and phone numbers
- Inventory outlining every item that is delivered
- Phone charger
- Water bottles for staff

- Floristry scissors
- Ribbon/fabric scissors
- Pliers
- Wire cutters
- Fold up table
- Apron/tool belt
- Dustpan and brush
- Dust sheet/oil cloth (waterproof)
- Pop-up garden waste bag for your green waste
- Small watering can or jug
- Long-reach refillable lighter (if you are providing candles and are insured to light them)

- Wires
- Twine
- Reel wire
- Spare ribbons
- Metal pins (for buttonholes)
- Pot tape
- Paper tape
- Florist's tape (waxed paper tape)
- Rope
- Hook-and-loop strapping (Velcro)
- Non-slip mat (useful for keeping designs such as funeral work, meadow boxes and mantelpiece arrangements in place)
- Pulleys (if required)
- Screwdriver/spanner/Allen keys and fixings if required for structures used in installations
- Ladders
- Tent pegs and ropes in case of windy weather if you are installing installations outside

Resources

Alternative products on the market aimed at reducing the need for single-use plastics

Holly Chapple Pillows and Eggs - Armatures made from 100% recyclable and reusable material (www.syndicatesales.com)

Flora Guppy - Floral arrangement holder (www.floraguppy.com)

Eco Fresh Bouquet Wraps - 100% biodegradable and compostable Floral Hydration Stem Sponge-Wrap™ System (www.ecofreshbouquet.com)

DIY Floral Grid - Reusable supportive grid structure (www.46spruce.com)

Tools that we use

Niwaki x Sakagen Flower Snips, Scissors and Secateurs (www.niwaki.com)

Sourcing Local Flowers

UK (www.flowersfromthefarm.co.uk)
A multi award-winning, not for profit, cooperative of British cut flower growers. Visit their website if you are looking for flower growers in the UK.

Ireland (www.flowerfarmarsofireland.ie)

France (www.collectifdelafleurfrancaise.com)

US (www.localflowers.org)

US and Canada (www.slowflowers.com)

US and worldwide (www.floretflowers.com/directory)

Australia (www.consortumbotanicus.com.au)

Further Sources of Information on Working Sustainably

'Eco Friendly Florists and Flower Growers Collective' Facebook Group (worldwide)

@nofloralfoam on Instagram - Raising awareness about plastic floral foam and alternative techniques for the flower community.

Sustainable floristry network (www.sustainablefloristry.org) – A global initiative guided by a collective of experienced florists working towards a more sustainable industry.

Books we have found useful or inspiring

Dictionary of Floristry and Flower Arranging.
Gattrell, A. (1988)

Constance Spry Handbook of Floristry.
Piercy, H. (1985)

The New Concise British Flora.
Martin, W. K. Kent, D. H. HRH The Duke of Edinburgh. (1991)

Plant Systematics
Simpson, M. (2010)

The British Flowers Book
Brown, C. (2018)
thebritishflowersbook.co.uk

The Floret Farm's Cut Flower Garden: Grow, Harvest, and Arrange Stunning Seasonal Blooms.
Benzakein, E. (2017)

Discovering the Folklore of Plants,
Baker, M. (2008)

About the Authors

Sarah Diligent is the owner of Floribunda Rose Floral Design, a high-end wedding and event studio in Hampshire, England. She approaches floral design in a sustainable way, celebrating seasonal British flowers and foliage, creating wedding florals and teaching sustainable floristry.

Sarah is passionate about change in an industry that is at its very heart a celebration of nature and she believes in minimising the carbon footprint of floristry without compromising quality. For her this book is the guide that she was looking for when she launched her business in 2014.

In 2018, Sarah launched 'The Eco Friendly Florists and Flower Growers Collective' and soon realised that she was not alone in looking for sustainable answers to unsustainable floristry practice.

Later that year she met William Mazuch while they were each designing installations for New Covent Garden Flower Market's British Flowers Week. Soon after meeting they realised that they shared a passion for British flowers and sustainable floral design, and within a few months of meeting they began work on A Guide to Floral Mechanics.

In 2017, William fell into the world of floral design by chance. Having trained in product design at Central Saint Martins in London before working on a range of product design projects, he approaches floral design with the mindset of an industrial designer, creating research-driven installations.

He found floral design appealing in a different way to industrial design; curating a moment which by its nature was short-lived, the sole purpose of which was to impart joy, contrasted starkly with his previous work.

Ever intrigued by botany and taking cues from the scents, forms and textures found in nature, William found the immediacy of working with natural, transient materials liberating. It was the foundation for a love of floral design.

While embarking on this new career he collected literature on the subject from all around the world to better understand how to work with flowers. It was at that point that William and Sarah's paths crossed.

Thank you

Our growers for inspiring us.
Our supportive families.
The organizers of British Flowers Week 2018, New Covent Garden Flower Market, and the Garden Museum, without whom we'd not have met.
Shane Connolly, for his support and encouragement.
Editor Kate Cullen.
Charlie Mills, and the rest of the team at Optichrome.
Sophia O'Connor for her portraits of us.
The people who tested our guides.

Each and every person who backed our crowdfunding campaign.

• 2lips florists • A Beautiful Occasion • A Curious Arrangement • À la Bonne Femme • Abbie Kennard-Jones • Abigail's Flower Truck • Adelaide Menzies • Adelaide's Secret Garden • Adele Blewett • Adele Miller • Adelle Irving-Guthrie • Agata Zwolińska • Agnieszka Manzi • Ailsa van Rooyen • Alana Watts | Petal and Wild • Alanna Drawson • Albelisa Kemp | Maple Field Floral • Alec Avakian • Alessia Borghetto • Alex Halliday • Alexander Hales | No.21 Flowers • Alexandra Chamness | Zoe + Aster • Alexandra Griffiths • Alexandra Herrero Maestra Floral • Alexandra Highet | Forever Wildfield • Alexandra Sterritt • Alexandra Stringer • Ali Spencer | Grace & Ray Flowers • Alice • Alice | Alice's flowers & designs • Alice | Wandering Violet Floristry • Alice Blue Collective Alice Holder • Alice Howard | Botanique Workshop • Alice May Flowers • Alice T • Alice Vine Floral Design • Alicia Larriera | Form Over Function • Alicia Tennant • Alison Cooper | The Flower Studio Manchester • Alison Johnson • Alison Norris • Alison Slater | frances&rose • Alison Trezies • Alison Trimmer | Fleuralis • Alliumflorist | Karen Copper • Ally Wright • Althea Wiles • Alva Orren Fen Cherry • Alys Holder • Amanda Burnette • Amanda McLean • Amanda Powell • Amanda Seales • Amanda Taffinder • Amber • Amber Flack • Amber Jean Flowers • Amber Persia • Amber Tapping • Amber Tritabaugh • Amelia Raben • Amelia Stubbs • Amy Bryant • Amy de Rohan-Truba • Amy Evans • Amy Florrister • Amy Kerton • Amy Shephard • Ana Kokoszko | Halls Florals • Ana Tonegaru | Pastel • Anchorage Floral | Anchorage Alaska USA • Andie Duthie • Andrea O'Donnell • Andri Benson • Angela & Alys • Angela Bateman • Angela Brooke-Smith • Angela Coulton | Petal and Twig • Angela Divincenti • Angela Lambert • Angela Lester • Angela Yeates • Angèle Noel • Angie | The Cottage Flower Farm • Angie Dodd • Anh • Anita | Bellinger Larrard Flowers • Anita Chillmaid • Ann P. Reid | BOTANIC • Ann Simpson • Ann Webbley | St Mary's Weston Turville • Anna • Anna Bell • Anna Fern Weddings • Anna Forster • Anna Jeon • Anna Marie Fitzgerald • Anna Potter | Swallows & Damsons • Anna Reddings | Tales From Apple Tree House • Anna Stretton | Babiana Botanic • Anna Truessel • Anna's Country Flowers • Annabel Jennings • Annabelle Hickson • Annabelle Rose • Anne Benfield • Anne Corrance Monk • Anne Oberwalleney | Ikoflowers • Anne Prenelle • Anne Vos • Anne Wanstall • Anne-Marie Knight | Spring Wood Flowers • Anneka Brown • Annie Kavanagh • Annie Lade • Annmarie Meyers • Anouchka Lototzky • Anthea Birden • Anthology Floral Design • Antoine • Anton Wijk • April Hernandez • Arianna Marinelli • Art and flora • Arthur B. Bacul • Ashleigh Aubrey •Ashley & Michelle | Green House Floristry • Ashley Anderson | Florage & Co. • Ashley Kirnan | Tarry Grove flower farm & design • Asti Shabrina • Atelier Aimer • atelier romance • Audrey Cecil • Avodah Living | Eva Monnier • Aya Ito/Petit Jardin de Fleurs • B B Abbott • BÄRA trädgård • Barbara McGhee • Barbara Urbanic • Barbora Martin • Barbs Coughtrey • Bbonnie • Beans and Blooms • Becca Franklin • Becks • Becky Branch | Branch and Bloom • Becky Feasby | Prairie Girl Flowers • Becky Hindley • Becky Smithson • Becky Woodcock • Bee Happy • Beehaven Flowers • Bekki Pierce • Belinda Campopiano • Bella Terra Flower Farm • Benita Tscharke • Berit Ødegård • Bespoke Flowers by Hanna • Beth Stewart • Bethan Hughes • Bettie Rose Flowers • Between The Briars | Irish flower farm + floristry • Bex | Botanical Tales • Beyond the Bloom • Billie Thomas • Birdwood & Willow • Black Rooster Farm, Kentucky USA • Blaise Drummond • Blend | Donna Carley • BLOOM BOY • Bloomantic • Blooming Divine • Bloomingayles • Bloomologie Flowers • Bloomsbay • BluBelle Creative • Bluebells & Daisies | Gemma • Bonnie Blooms • Boom Blooms • Boujdi Veronique • Boyes Botanics • Bramble & Wild • Bramshill Flowers • Branch And West Floral • Brancoprata • Brave Botanics • Brenda Murphy • Brian Watson • Bridget Tierney • Brigitte Girling | Moss & Stone Floral Design • Bronwyn E Chandler • Brooke Hanstock • Bryony Mae Flowers • Bud & Bee • Bumblebee Flower Farm • bunchesofhappiness.co.uk • Camilla Gulbrandsen • Cara Heggie • Carina K • Carla Morey • Carla Pavincich | The Ivy League • Carly Convey | Conveys Petal House • Carly Coulter • Carol | Branch and Bloom NZ • Carol King • Carol Siddorn • Carola Puddy-Henny | The Sunflower Lady • Carole Stanley • Carolina Vieira Ly • Caroline • Caroline Bishop • Caroline Elkington • Caroline Fleetwood@fledgling_flowers • Caroline Hodges Flowers • Caroline J Hooper • Caroline Linares • Caroline Nangle Brereton • Caroline Oden & Jules Cossins | Where Inspiration Blooms • Caroline Polden Flowers • Caroline Thompson • Caroline Wilson • Carolle | Rambling Rose • Caron Heath • Carrie | Rose and Thorns • Casa Selva • Cassandra Sansosti • Cassie Cannon • Caswell Flower Company • Cat Allen • Cate Wood | Flowers at 180 - Mirfield • Cath Kenny @ CatkinBlooms • Cath Roberts • Catherine | Elworthy Flowers • Catherine Burton • Catherine Daly • Catherine Duncan • Catherine Godek • Catherine Jackson • Catherine Sharrem | Gathered Floral • Catherine Traynor | Snapdragon Edinburgh • Cathryn Whiteside Florals Hampshire | The Village Florist in North Waltham • Cathy Crozier-Cole | Umbel • CC's Blooms • Céline| Fleur de Carotte • Charlie Armour | Wild at Heart, N. Somerset • Charlie Price • Charlotte and Will •

• Chan Zhi Shan • Charlotte Argyrou | Botanical Illustrator • Charlotte Forster • Charlotte Wood | Wild Wood London • Chirsty • Chirsty Macaulay • • Chloë Meredith • Chris Pearce • Chrissie Leader • Chrissy Barnes • Chrissy Stables • Christa Ory • Christa Stosiek • Christien Schrecker • Christina Natale • • Christina Yan • Christine Pemberton • Christine Polyzos • Cindy Devacht • Cindy Gilbert | Bloom Floral Boutique • Cirkel Studio Linda Karlsson • • Cissy @_wildstems_• City Blossoms LV • Claire | Fig and Fern • Claire Brown | Plantpassion • Claire Clark | Pear Tree House Flowers, Ilkley • Claire de lis • • Claire MacIver • Claire Slater • Claire Sylvester • Claire Waddington • Clara Barthorp | Wilde Thyme • Clare Arthur | Hendra Farm Flowers • • Clare Mannion • Clare Wilder | Clementine Moon Floral Design • Clementines Wedding and Event Floristry • Clifton Flowers • Coco Pear • Colin Chuter • • contact@capucine-atelier-floral.fr • Corina Schurman • Coseytown Flowers • Cotswold Country Flowers • Creature Comfort Flowers • Cristina Colli • • Cristina Herbert • Crystal Carroll • Curzon Tussaud • Cynthia Maylane Luong Gerbore • D Watts • D.Broekhuizen • Daisy Cosmos • Daisy Works • • Damson & Vine Floral Design • Dandelions and Grace • Daniel Cook • Daniela Moncada • David Inge • Dawn • Dawn Clements Floral Couture • • Days of Dahlia • Debbie Chalet • Debbie Reeves • Debbie Taylor • Debby Mittelman • Dedicated to Helga Loeb • Dee Kelly • Delamere Flower Farm • • Della Indradi • Denise Carson • Denise Gale • Désirée fleurs • Desmond Chua • Diana | Go Floral • Diana Barnes • Diana Basurto • Diana Mitcham • • Diane Quick • Dianna | Red Lavender Floristry • Dianne Axe • Die Retter der Tafelrunde • Dittany Entwined floral design • Dominique • • Dominique Erichsen • Dominique Northam • Dr Sarah K Cook • East Kent Flower Company • East Lothian Flower Farm • Edel Noone • • Eden Frei | Garden of Eden Floral Design • Édua Décore • Edwards Flowers • Edythe Ann Borràs Rhodes • Eileen Herlihy • Marcus Ekström • Elaine Freer • • Elder & Wild • Eleanor Hadlow • Eleanor Harwood-Todd • Eli McDonald • Elisabeth Coulson • Elise C • Elise Moriceau | Fleurettes • Elizabeth Adams • Elizabeth Boothroyd • Elizabeth Fancourt • Elizabeth Grundy • Elizabeth Jones • Elizabeth Sawyer • Elizabeth Simpson | In-a-Gadda-Da-Vida Flowers • • Elle-Rose Dunn • Ellen Kenny • Ellen Millhollon • Ellen Montelius • Ellen Seagraves | Chic Florals • Ellen Wilson • Ellermann Flower • • Ellie | Rock Sea Floral Design • Ellie Cannon • Ellie Jones • Elna Nilsson • Elsa Marcel • Elyse Griffin • Elysia Schultz • Em • Emilie Timmermans • • Emily Cooper • Emily Cooper • Emily Hen • Emily Hepworth | Persephone Violet • Emily Hewitt | Wilderness • Emily Jensen • Emily Stolting • • Emily Talling | Three Acre • Emily Wisher • Emily Wykes • Emma @ELK Creations • Emma | Urban Flower Farmer • Emma Cabrera | Tigers to Lilies • • Emma Canning • Emma Cox • Emma Davies • Emma Dodson • Emma Dunlop • Emma Edkins • Emma Gittings • Emma Guyot-Prémel • Emma Hewlett • • Emma Lawson • Emma McDonald | Stems • Emma Parkinson • Emma Powell • Emma Thistlethwaite • Emma Whitworth • Érica Carvalho • • Erica Crawford • Estelle Flowers • Esther • Eucalyptus Paris - florist • Eveline's Flowers • Evergreen Floral Design • Extrafloral • Eydís Ósk Ásgeirsdóttir • • F. Cannon • FAB Floral & Stems • Faith Brennan | Le Coeur Sauvage • Farm to Floral • Farrell's Nursery IRL • Feather Grass Florals • Felicity Jones • • Felicity Kendall • Fester L.D. MacKrell • Field & Floret • Fierceblooms and her Cheshire Canalside Cutting Garden • Fiona Ball • Fiona Blacklock • • Fiona Closier • Fiona Haser Bizony • Fiona Hay • Fiona Perry • Fiona Pickles | Firenza Flowers • Fiona West | Like the Moon in Daytime • Fiona Young • • Fionnuala Mc Auley | Scarecrow Flowers • FIORETTI Paris • Fiorificio Italy • Fioritura | Ciera Schmid • Fireside Farm NC • Fleur Provocateur • • Flora & Daisy | Peldon • Flora Fricker • FloraFern Florist Designer • Floral Acre • floralatelier.es • Florbero Floral Gift Studio • Flore Vallery Radot • • Floreando Ando | Patricia Marañon • Floren Studio • Floristeria Picris • Floro Folio • Flos Botanical Studio • Flourish Floristry • • Flourish Sussex Flower School • Flowercap • Flowermug • Flowerpower Budapest • Flowers & Moods • Flowers and the Moon • • Flowers by Alexandra Grace • Flowers by Minty, Edinburgh • Flowers by Ola • Flowers Evolution • Flowers from the Garden Huddersfield • Flowersmiths • • Flying Little Birds • Foliage and Fern Floral Design • Forbes Flower Farm Alford • Fox & Petal Floral Design • Foxglove Studio | Lucie Wixon-Ellis • • Fran and the Flower • Frances and Mary | Horsley Flowers • Frances Boscawen • Frances Rawson | Clodhopper Blooms • Franniefloral • • Franny Brown Florist • Franziska Zacharias • Frau Franzz • Freesia & Fox • From Garden to Vase - Northamptonshire • Future Flower Farm • • Gabriela Queiróz Ferreira • Gabriella • Gabrielle Norén • Gaia Eros (born Elkington) • Gail Bennett • Garden Gate Flowers • Garden of England Flowers • • Garden to Garland • Gay Francis • Gemma | Ultramarine • Gemma Blaskey • Gemma Burniston • Gemma Guilfoyle • Gemma Hales • Gemma Kelsall • • Gemma Quinton Floral Design • Georgia Guglielmucci • Georgina Chapman Flowers • Gill | Into the Blooms • Gill Baque • Gill Stewart • Gill stone • • Gill Tate • Gillian Brown • Gillian Neild • Giulia Repetti | Cascina Brontola • Gorton & Granger • Grace & Violet • Grace and Flowers • • Grace Koh En Hui • Graeme Corbett | Bloom + Burn • Green and Gorgeous • Green Daisy • Gretel • @grownandforagedgatherings • Guy Mazuch • • Gyan Gurung • Gyongyi Somlai • H M S Floristry | Heidi Marie Shuttle • H P Jones • H Shelton • Haemin.K • Hana Moss Flowers • Hanako Flowers • • Hannah • Hannah Blunt • Hannah Cheeseman • Hannah Hunnam • Hannah Jackson _thegardenofevie_ • Hannah Lister | Blossom + Ash • • Hannah Mary Ford • Hannah Maynard • Hannah Streeter • Hannah Tiedeman • Harold Forster • Harriet Parry Flowers • Harriet Pound-Jones • • Harriet Smithson | Cumberland Flower Farm • Harsimran Kaur Jagdev • Hattie Price • Hay Lane Flowers • Hayley Evans • • Hayley Gee | Cacti & Wildflower • Hayloft & Hedgerow • Haze Lea Designs | Katherine Jones • Heather Mullen • Heather R Hanselmann • • Heather Snodgrass-Brine | Popette Studio • Heidi Duffy MBE • Heledd Hughes • Helen Baxter • Helen Blewitt • Helen Cho • • Helen Cushnie • Helen Faulkner • Helen Godfrey • Helen Land • Helen Main Ellen • Helen Sarah Vaughan • Helen Sharpe • Helen Sheard • Helen Suich • • Helen Vincent • Helena Melander • Helene Deudon • Helga Loeb • Hen Dy Garden Flowers • Heritage Farm Florals • Hilary Dickson • Hilary Pattison • • Hollie Freeland • Hollie White • Holly • Holly & Gary Floral Art Devon • Holly Brookins • Homefield Flowers • Honeymoon Fern • • Honeysuckle & Hilda • Howe Farm Flowers • Howe Hill Flower Farm • I ♥ U Tamara W • Iain & Hat Smith • Ickybana • Imogen Yusko • • In dedication to Pamela Davis • India Hurst • Indre Norvaisaite | Nothing but flowers • Inessa Nichols • Ingrid Laurenson • Iona Kendall • • Iris Hildur Eriksdottir • Isabel Page • Isabella Thorndike Church • Isla Fitridge | Scout's Garden • Island Bride Flowers • IXIA Botanicals • Jacinta Young • • Jackie Barden • Jackie Brooks • Jaclyn Lott • Jacqueline Franklin | Hope and Glory Flower Company • Jaicelyn Rowe • Jala Goikoetxea • JamJam • • Jan Jenkins • Jana Teteris • Jane | The Floral Nest • Jane Allan • Jane Brinkerhoff • Jane E Oei • Jane Farthing | Daphne and Doreen Flower Studio • • Jane Gandon | Bicycle Blooms • Jane Lester • Jane Millar • Jane Segar • Jane Sked-Connop • Jane Wenman • Jane Williams • Jane-Ann Walton • • Janet Mary Floral Design • Janet Wilde | Wilde & Romantic • Janice Palmer | Yorkshire Petals • Janne Ford • Jasmine & Jerusalem | Alexandra Stephenson • • Jaune Pivoine • Jaymie Evans • Jayne Caithness • Jayne Eaton • Jayne Solomon • Jazzy Oliver • Jean Orpwood • Jen | Goldfinch Floral Studio • Jen Czaja • • Jen DeMarti | Urban Marigold Floral Design • Jen Prosser | JenniBloom Flowers • Jennifer Scholle • Jennifer Scholle • Jennifer Schuitema • Jenny Casey • • Jenny Dixon • Jenny Fleur • Jenny King • Jenny Lord • Jenny Mugford • Jenny Peters • Jenny White • Jess Bourgeois • Jess Wheeler • Jessica Aldsworth • • Jessica Davies • Jessica Höglund • Jessica Roberts • Jessica Smith | Flower & Land | Floral Designer, Grower and Gardener • Jessica Woodrow • • Jill Brennan | Isla and me • Jill Houston | Little Park Flowers • Jill Slater • Jo Cox • Jo Drake | Clock Dandelion • Jo Frost Flowers • Jo Pegues • • Jo Williams | Issy & Bella Floral Design • Joan Connolly • Joan Holmes | Floral Flowers & Foliage • Joann Cook • Joanna • Joanne Brook • Joanne Truby •

• Jodie Craven | Bee Croft Blooms • Jodie Farrell • Jodie Hamilton • Jodie Vigor | Boutique Blooms • Johanna Gates • Johanna Pedrick Flowers • • Jolie de Miranda • Jonathan and Vivian Haines • Joolz Abbs-Woodd • Jori Krenzel | Floral Designer • Jos Sheffield • Josephine Dreßler • Judith Rhind-Tutt • • Judy Cranham • Judy Scott • Judy Ward • Jules Morrell | Elderberry Flower Company • Jules Paice • Juli Vaughn Designs • Julia Campbell • • Julia Lynn Floral Design • Juliana Bermingham • Julie Bircher | The Cutting Garden • Julie James • Julie Peace • Julie Vaughan • Julie White • • Juliet | Babylon Flowers • Juliet Medforth • Justdahlias | Philippa Stewart • Justine Baxter • Justine Stringer@generousgardener • K Kongsawat • K. Haulk • • Karen • Karen Ben Tolila Hilmersson • Karen Hughes | The Somerset Cut Flower Garden • Karen Ingall • Karen Lambert-Cox • Karen Lawson • • Karen Newman • Karen Watts | Petal and Bee • Karen Wibberley | Foxgloves and Lillies • Kari Pedersen • Kat Crossley • Kat Szabo • Kate Adamson • • Kate Brown • Kate Brunton Broughton • Kate Carpenter • Kate Collyer • Kate Cullen • Kate Ellis • Kate Gardner • Kate Geyle Flowers • Kate Glassock • • Kate Gordon Lennox • Kate Ladd | greenery • Kate Mackay | Floral Park • Kate Neech | Mrs Neech's Flowers • Kate Read • Kate Robinson • • Kate Symington • Kate Werry | Ministry of Flowers • Kate White Hamilton • Kate Wilson • Katharine Clarke • Katherine Birtles • • Katherine Craft | Florist in the Forest • Katherine Fry • Katherine Hoke • Katherine Nee • Katherine Whitworth | Fieldgardenflowers • • Kathryn & Lorna | Skylark Flower Company • Katie | BLWM Flowers • Katie Day • Katie Ebbs • Katie Hobbs • Katie Isitt | Kidge Flowers • • Katie McHardy • Katie Musgrave • Katie Scales • Katy Drinkwater Bieniosek • Katy Sutor • Kayla Egert • Kayleigh Sanderson | Astilbe & Rose • • Kaytee Stice | Roots Floral Design • Keeping the Plot • Kelly Hosanna Chai • Kelly Minns | Delphi Flowers • Kelsey Gray Events • Kemlo and Kemlo • • Kendall Platt | Adventures with Flowers • Kensington flowers • Kerin Greville • Kerry | The Freelance Florist • Kerry Ashby • • Kerry Bellamy | Cotswold Flower Design • Kerry Bushe • Keythorpe Walled Garden • Keziah Newlove • Khadijeh H S Masty • Kim Butler • • Kim Dawkins | Pig Pen Flowers • Kim Hye Jin • Kim Turtle • Kim Zimmerman | Rowdy Poppy in Denver, CO • Kirsten Abbott • • Kirsten Mackay | Henthorn Farm Flowers • Kirsty | The Wilde • Kirsty McCormick • Krista McCallum | Pick This Farm & Studio • Kristen • • Kristen Primrose • Kristin Brown • Kristine • Kristyn Kok | @boxingblooms Malaysia • Krystle Simms | Poppykock • LABOOS Flowers • • Lady Garden Flowers • Ladyfern Flowers • Lakshmi Gollapalli • Lara Kenny - Love from lila xx • Larisa Minerva | Bewilder Floral • LarkinInBloom • • Laura Baaij • Laura Beale | Fern Cottage Floristry • Laura Dunkley • Laura Evans | Copper Bloom • Laura Grala • Laura Jones • • Laura Montgomery | Xyris Botanicals • Laura Sandiford • Laura Taylor | Green Earth Flowers • Laura Winslow | The Petal Pixie • • Lauren Farquhar and Rosie Flanagan • Laurita Arias • Lavender & Rose • Lavender and bee • Lavender View Farm • LD • Le Muguet Floral Design Studio • • Leah Busch | Spathe & Spade • Leah K. Gibson • Lee Moonjoo • Leeann Swarbrick • Leigh Chappell Flowers • Leilanie Shedden • Lennie Wall Wallflower • • Les Jolies Feuilles • Les Ombelles • Lesle Hill • Lesley Rutter • Lesley Stevenson • Lesley Worboys • Lexi Morris | Little & Wild Flowers • Libby Black • • Libby Holden • Libby Nairn Hands Full | Flowers Ullapool Scotland • Lillicreek Florals • Lilly Chen • Lily Hughes • Lily Jayne Florist • Lily's Florist | Alexandria • • Limewood Flowers • Linda Beardsley, in memory of my Mum Hazel Bray, who taught me to love flowers. • Linda Bradbury-Flint • Linda Clark • • Linda Dolan • Linda Warner | Country Blooms • Lindsay | Cornishcountrygardenflowerco • Lindsay Diminick | Yellow Twist Design • Lindsay Morrissey • • Lindsey Kennedy • Lindsey L Vandevier | Rosaspina Floral • Lins Renucci • Lisa Darban Bespoke Floristry, dedicated to the support of a sustainable floral industry! • Lisa King • Lisa Marie Grigsby | Down by the river florals • Lisa Nightingale • Lisa Oshea • Lisa Selvage • Lisa Waterson | The Enchanting Owl • • Lisel Vonhoff • Liz Inigo Jones • Liz Mathers-Carter | Flower & Fern • Liz Wilkinson • Liza Keane • Lizzie Cree • Lizzie Rhoda • Lizzie Thorne • • Lizzy Chambers • Lizzy Mobbs | The Southwold Flower Co • Lois Golding • Long Barn Flowers • Lorist the florist • Lottie Davis • Lou Fish • Lou Ord • • Louisa du Rose • Louise Crasky • Louise James Florist • Louise Langdon Florals • Louise McWatters • Louise Monaco • Louise Roberts • Louise Sampson • • Louises flower boutique • Louisina Currie • Lovely Bridal Blooms • Lovette Farm Flowers • Luce Loves Flowers • Lucia Braham • Lucie • Lucie Wixon-Ellis • • Lucinda Florence • Lucinda Tasker • Lucy Akerman • Lucy Beney | Bblooms • Lucy Day | Wild Bloom • Lucy Gumban • Lucy Mansfield • Lucy Nairn • • Lucy the Flower Hunter • Lush Events • Lydia Cywinski • Lyn Savage • Lyndal Gubbels • Lynette Oswin • Lynn Irvin | Ivy & Rose Flowers • • Lynne Robinson • M Leeves • M Santiago • Mad Lilies • Maddie McCormack • Made in Flowers, Kendal • Madhu Devi Ishaya • Madison Deffé • • Madison Razor • Madita-Grace and Flowers • Maggie Etheridge • Mandy Purvis • Manon Collard • Mara Kapsis • marcella@theparcelflower.co • • Márcia Wood • Margherita Tomba • Marguerite Legros • Mari Saarelainen | Taiga to Tropics • Maria | Sorori Design Florist • Maria D. Leon • • Maria del Carmen Garcia Megido • María del Pilar Currea Caballero • María Eugenia García-Quijada Luaces • Maria Ghansah • Maria Heywood • • Maria Thompson • Maria Vert-SempreViva • Maria@gioiasecretlab • Marian Castro-Mendivil Gubbins • Marian Wiltshire • Marianne Fowler • • Marianne Slater • Marica Hilton • Marie Kavanova • Mariia Adamanskaia | Miss Marta Studio • Marina Aguirre Lipperheide • Mariya Doncheva • • Marly Surena-Llorens • Martina | RAW Fleurs • Martina McEnroe • Martina Plantina • Mary Anne Crevasse • Mary Catherine Gallagher • Mary Cullen • • Mary Donnell • Mary Kelava • Mary M • Mary Smith | RubyBlooms • Marysia Wieckowska • Maryssa Dowe Floral Design • Masami Lavault • Matthew • • Matthew Landers • Maximilian • Mayfield Flowers Scotland • McConnell Blooms • Meg Shaw • Megan Woodhouse • Meinir Blunt • Mel Adams • • Melania Tandio • Melie Desbrosse • Melissa Githens | Flowers by Melly B • Melissa Lim • Melissa Pack • Melissa Pritchard • Meryl Clarke | Nodding Violets • • Michael Hirschl • Michela Savio • Michelle Anne Floristry for Superhero Alex ♥ • Michelle Davies • Michelle Hill • Michelle Joy Howard | Flora Couture • • Michelle Kanes • Michelle Kenstler • Michelle Palmer • Middleton Lodge Estate • Miho Camille Yoshimura • Mikaela Törnlind • Mimi Ivanovic • • Miranda Mewhort • Miranda Smith • Mirta Flower Farm | Martina Pagani • MMN Flowers • Moira MacKinnon • Molly Zager • Monet Floral Gallery • • Monica Acosta Sabater • Moody Blooms • Moonraker and Rose • Morgan Howell Moylan • Morgan Marie Jackson • Motler • Mrs Bee's Flower Co • • Murfy Stewart • myfloralstyling • Mylène Aurore Giroux • Myrtle Fox & Maude • Nadia Addonizio • Nancy Moon • Nancy S Weigandt • Nancy Wisot • • Naomi Drage • Naomi Hackwood • Naomi Hall | Blooms from the Barn • Natalia Carhartt • Natalia Galván Vila • Natalie Celuch • Natalie F • Natalie • • Lauraine English • Natalie Zemskaya • Natasha Morgan • Natasha Rodwell • Natasha Vass • Nathan Hokin • Natural Branscombe • • Nemori Flower Farm, Yass River, Australia • Nic Atkins • Nic Morgan • Nichole Johnston | Xo Design Co. Events • • Nicky Gaffney | The Stonegate Flower Company • Nicola Lovegrove • Nicola Porciani • Nicolas Guiné • Nicole Laird • Nicole Liew | The White Orchid • • Nicole Sonier- Hoe | Love, Life, & Joy Flowers • Nicole Steinmetz • Nina Blyth-Owen • Nina Horan • Nixie Pyrena • Nolan Allan • • Non Davies | Blodau'r Border Bach Flowers • Nordic Twigs Flowers & Styling • Northcombe Flowers • Northern Hands • NOSiOKO | Mari Neuschitzer • • Nunu Designs • Obvious State • Old Farmhouse Flowers, Lincs • Olga Campagnoli • Olga Grigoryeva | Lilas & Rose Floral Studio • • Olive James Bouquets Cohasset, MA USA • Olivemsy • Olivia Day | Everyday Flowers • Olivia Manson • Ona Rose • One Flew Over • • Orchard Farm Flowers • Orznash Blooms • Pam Glover • Pam Wittcomb | Croft Flowers • Paradise Blooms • Passionflowers by Emma Spowage • • Pati Duque • Paula Brasaanï • Paula Edgington • Paula Ellis | fox & thorn • Paula Hobson | Wildflowers & Moss • Paula Routledge • Paxxy & Flora •

• Pearsons School of Floristry • Penny Dommett | Plans & Plants • Penny Hall • Penny I'Anson • Penny Nichol • Pepy Keegan • Persephone Floral Atelier • • Peta Frost • petal & partridge • Petal & Stalk • Petal Decor | Jess and Charmaine • Petal Met Sugar • Pheasant Botanica • • Philippa Ferridge MFA Boston Floral design associate • Philippa Lawley-Barrett • Phytology Flowers • Pink and Rose Flowers • Pink Palms • Pip Bensley • • Pip Middleton • Pipley Flowers • Piri Cullimore • Pitfield Barn Cut Flower Farm & Studio • Plot 31 • Plukbloem.nl • Pollen Floral Joy • • Polly Morgans | Dewdrop Florals • Polly Nicholson • Poppy | Poppy Wild Floral • Poppy Sherborne • Posy & Tie Floral Design • Pretty Fix | Viv Wong • • Pretty Floral • Primula Floral Styling • Puggs Meadow Flowers • Queenie's Floral Design • Quinn Czejkowski • • Quinn's Blooms and Greenery, Cobourg, ON • Quirky Flowers • R. Schrenk • Rachael | Peony and Fern • Rachael Ashton • Rachael Hardy | The Love Garden • • Rachael Kennedy • Rachel Fletcher • Rachel Hounsome | Rae's Boutique • Rachel Petheram • Rachel Vater • Raynor Sumner • • Reagan Johnson | Copper + Bloom Floral • Rebecca Day • Rebecca Goff • Rebecca Hosken • Rebecca Hough • Rebecca Mays • Rebecca Morgan • • Rebecca Morris • Rebecca Reeves • Rebecca Sant • Rebecca Stolz • Rebecca Tappin • Rebecca Warne • Rebecca Yussuf | Lilac and Lace Floral Design • • Rebeccah Stripling • Rebekah Ellis • Rebekah Rixon | Headley Flower Garden • Rebel and the Rose • Red Eden & Olive • Reichei Tan • Renee Carver • • Reverie Fields, Boulder Colorado • Ria Mishaal • Richard • Richard Haslam • Richard Mazuch • Rita Levitt • Robin Berta • Robyn Beacom • • Robyn Paulin | The Black Peony • Robyns Nest Floral Design • Rona Wheeldon | Flowerona • Roos Truwant • Rora • Ros Claase • Rosalind Bennett • • Rosalind Rosewarne Jenkins • Rosalind Yates • Rosamund Bryar • Rose Ottley | A Pocketful of Roses • Rose Talbot • Rosemary | Ammi Styling Ltd • • Rosemary Lanning • Rosie Conroy | Lavender & Rose • Rosie Gray | Galloway Flowers • Rosie Naish • Rosie O'Connor • Rosie Winder • Rosie Winter • • Rowena Westhead • Rox & Rose • Roz Saggers • Ruby & Grace Florist • Ruby Foxglove • Running Wild Flowers • Ruth Alder | Flowersmith • Ruth Bowen • Ruth Fagg • • Ruth Hyland • Ruth Moushabeck | Etheldreda Floral • Ryan Lewis | Bloom by Ryan Lewis • S Trefusis • S&A Floral Design • Sacha Przewieslik-Allen • • Safia Dahhan • Sahra Rayner • Sally Anne Maile • Sally Groves | Bloomthyme • Sally McMillan • Sally Morgan • Sally Reeves • Sally Wragg • • Saltbox&Co • Sam | Fantail Designer Florist • Sam Dickenson • Sam Hunter • Sam Hutson • Samantha Hutson • Sammie Barton • Sammy Hartley • • Samuel Andersson • Sandra Bright • Sandro Meier • Sandy Ingham • Santacata Flores • Sara Louise Coleman • Sara Nicholls • • Sara Redman | The Flower Meadow • Sara Willman | My Flower Patch, Wiltshire, UK • Sarah | Flower Pasture • Sarah | The Flower Press Blog • • Sarah | The Petal Emporium • Sarah Buteux • Sarah Dempster • Sarah Elizabeth Duggan • Sarah Felix • Sarah French • Sarah Good • • Sarah Hammond | English Peonies, Norfolk • Sarah Landers • Sarah Langlais • Sarah Levine • Sarah Lewis • Sarah Lunstrum | Dream Farm Flowers • • Sarah Nixon • Sarah Penny Flowers • Sarah Richardson Leafy Couture • Sarah Shuttle • Sarah Statham | Simply By Arrangement • Sarah Trevatt • • Sarah Whiting | Nettlewood Flowers • Sarah Wilson | Compton Garden Flowers • Sarah Wyatt | Treasured Bouquets • Saskia Vegter • • Sea Change Farm & Flower • Seana's Flowers • Sebastian Conrad • Seekings Flower Farm • Selah Lodge • SES • Shan Sherwood • Shane J G Connolly • • Shanoah LaPatka | Shakopee Florist • Sharon • Sharon Jackson • Sharon Lake • Sharon Pointen • Sheila Fitzgerald | A New Leaf, Omaha, Nebraska • • Sheila Hume | Blue Hen Flowers • Sheila Louise Melville • Sheila McCook-Weir, to commend the flower ladies of Blockley Parish Church, Gloucestershire • • Shelagh Macartney • Sherly Wiryasaputra • Shirley & Hong • Shirley Doherty • Shirley Sanderson • Shona McTaggart • Siân Swinton • Siân Wild • • Silver Thread Gardens • Silvia Meyer • Simon Lycett • Simone Torpey | The Little Urban Flower Farm, Australia • Sioux Nixon • Smokebush Floral Design • • Sofia Nilsson • Soh Fia • Sonia Marshall • Sonya Read • Sophie Barker • Sophie Berry • Sophie Birt Floral Design • Sophie Brennan • Sophie Bromley • • Sophie Eley • Sophie Firth | Lily & Larkspur • Sophie George • Sophie Leathart • Sophie Roberts • Sophie Schlachter • Sophie Walker Walsh • • Sophie Warren-Smith • Sophie Wiking • Sorcha Herbert • Sow Pretty • Spring Wind Farm • Stamford Flowers | Siobhan Bryant • Stella Turner Floral • Stems Brooklyn • • Steph | Rabbit and the Rose • Stephanie Dixon • Stephanie Ho • Stephanie Roseanne Design • Stephen & Petrina Miles • Stephen Allen • • Stina M Skogqvist • Studio Seapink • Style Your Spaces • Sue Biggs • Sue Chapman • Sue Huggett • Sue Pardon • Sue Powell • • Sue Roberts | Cecilia Hill Floral Design, USA • Sue White • sue@suearranflowers.com • Sundari Uthayakumar • Sungrove Blossoms Flowers and Events • • Surprised by Joy • Susan Byram • Susan McLeary • Susanna Todd • Susanne Loweth | Beamsley Blooms • Susie Weedon • Suzanne Hunbert • • Suzanne Walker | Little Tin Shed Flowers • Suzie Meers • Svante • Sweet Afton Floral • Sybil Dodds | Valued friend, support and floristry teacher • • Sylvia Abraham • Sylvie Huigen • Tallulah Rose Flower School • Tammie Lefevre LaBonte • Tamsin McCabe • Tanya Shaw | Oh Flora Studio • • Tanya Siska • Tanya Steinhauser | Seakale Floral Art & Design • Taryn Cullen Humphrey • Tattie Rose • Teresa Cheung • Teresa Moss • Teresa Wheeler • • Tessa | Fox and Thistle Floral Designs • Tessa Mecham • Thanh-Ha Florentin • The Bath Flower School • The Bell Jar Flowers • The Blackbird Garden • • The Caithness Bunch • The Clarkes • The Cotswold Garden • The Floral Fairy • The Flower Folk • The Flower Keep | Jennifer Savzyan • • The Flower Pavilion • The Flower School St Albans • The Foraged Flower Co. • The Forgotten Garden • The Golden Letter • The lavender hill company • • The Noosa Flower Box, Queensland, Australia • The Petal Girl • The Posy Patch • The Redwood Florist • The Seasonal Flower Co. • • The Self Cultivated Woman • The Stem-ery • The Stockbridge Flower Company | For Isla and Cameron • The Summerhouse • The Sussex Flower School • • The Wild One's Floristry • The Woodland Farm • Thea Stokes • There May Be Bugs | Annie Jenkins • Thomas Off • Tia & Green • Tia Robson • • Tide Flowers • Tienfeng Chang • Tiffany Kightley • Tiggy Johnson • Tinna Bjarnadóttir • Tjikko Floral • Tom Gyr | tomsstudio • Tom-Andre Fredriksen • • tomtom • Toni Crowther • Toria Britten | Wildly Beautiful Flowers • Tracey Bell | Ruebury Flowers • Tracey Bridger • Tracey Graham • • Tracey Morris | ella & louie flowers • Tracey Mosley • Tracy Beaumont • Tracy McDermott | The Good Life Blooms • • Treea Cracknell | The London Flower Farmer • Tricia Ferguson flowers • Tricia Jones • Trish Carter | Blue Mountains Floral Designs • Troy Vimalasatya • • Twig & Bo Florist | S. Davies • Twisted Sisters • Twisted Tulip Designs • Under the Laurel Tree • Val Donaldson • Vanessa de Lande Long • Vanessa Gallach • • Vanessa Jayne Design • Vanessa Swetman • Vic English from Telopea Flowers • Vick Thornton | Blooming Lovely Flowers and Plants • Vickey Robinson • • Vicki Fleury • Victoria Evans • Victoria Gaiger • Victoria O'Quin • Victoria Taberer Bond • Victoria Zhuk • Vinabloemen • Viola Johansson • • Violet & Vine • Violet + Wylde • Violeta Gladstone • Vivian Cooper • Vivienne Rowden • Wanda Aasen • We are Wildflowers • Wendy Hammersley • • Wendy Paul | Organic Blooms • Wendy Porritt • Wessex Flower Company • When Frankie Met George • Whispers & Snippets • • Whitney Schedeler | The Story Of Flowers • Wild and Chic • Wild Botanicals Floral Design • Wild Flora Studio • Wild Florals • • Wild Rose Flower Company • Wild Rose Flowers • Willow & Wildflower • Willow Crossley • Willowbrook Flowers • Xantiana Young • Yun Hsuan Niu • • Yvette Willson • Zanda Bhogal • Zandy Russell • Zetia Dennis • Zoë Davies | Love Wild • Zoe Field • Zoë Horsfield • Zoe's Little Flower Farm •

Thank you to the six anonymous backers who also supported us.